A Vision for You

With our love
Geeco

Geeco Publishing

First Published Amazon Kindle 2024

www.geecopublishing.com

ISBN: 978 1 0687672 0 3

Disclaimer

Also published by Geeco

Enjoy In Joy

A Simple Way

Escape to Joy

Tradition 12

"Anonymity is the spiritual foundation of all our traditions,
ever reminding us to place principles before personalities."

This book was created by the joint efforts of the members of
Geeco, and we are equal creators. We offer it to you under
our collective name, Geeco.

Many thanks to Autumn Hardacre and Jack Moberg
for their encouragement and editorial assistance

**If you enjoy the messages in this book,
please help us get them out into the world
by leaving a review on Amazon.**

Enjoy

Learning

The whole purpose of education is to turn mirrors into windows.

Sydney J Harris

We get it wrong, make mistakes, wallow in shame, and talk to ourselves about how we have failed – again!

I want to suggest that we discard all those ways of judging ourselves.

From now on, whenever we "make a mistake", we view it as a "learning experience".

It is a stepping stone to achieving, becoming, and being the person we want to be.

You may still need to have that "learning experience" many times. If that is so, keep clocking them as learning experiences.

One day, it will change, and you will change.

Be kind and loving to yourself.

He who learns but does not think, is lost! He who thinks but does not learn is in great danger.

Confucius

A man who asks is a fool for five minutes. A man who does not ask is a fool for life.

Chinese Proverb

January 2

Happiness

There is only one happiness in life, to love and be loved.

George Sand

Think about something or someone in your life that makes you happy, and realise the power of that feeling.

To ensure you've got this, think of something else that makes you happy and feel that happiness throughout your body. Relish the comfort that comes with that.

Happiness is the people and the things in your life that you love.

Now, think about something you really "desire," the thing you would buy or get today if you could. Imagine the feeling you get from this.

It is not happiness. It lacks the completeness of happiness. You may think it will make you happy, but the feeling that comes with desire is different.

By and large, the things we desire do not make us happy. They are just the sugar coating that comes with their arrival. The lie is that they will "fill the hole." They seldom do.

Happiness comes from what we already have in our lives.

Happiness cannot be travelled to, owned, earned, worn or consumed. Happiness is the spiritual experience of living every minute with love, grace, and gratitude.

Denis Waitley

People need to realise that true happiness comes from self-development, not self-indulgence.

Jeffrey Fry

January 3

Anxiety

Anxiety is love's greatest killer. It makes others feel as you might when a drowning man holds onto you. You want to save him, but you know he will strangle you with his panic.

Anais Nin

Anxiety can creep, or even land fully formed, into our lives and our being. Instantly diminishing us.

Our future or present worries about our children or parents, the job market, property prices, the latest illnesses, the traffic jam, all or any of them, can crush us with anxiety.

And by and large, there is nothing we can do about them. Oh, sorry, yes, we can. We can turn up our anxiety levels and feel even worse. But that's not doing anything about them. It's just doing something to ourselves.

Is there anything that you can do right now that will alter or improve the situation?

If there is, you can choose to do it.

If there is not, let go of it.

And travel forward beyond the event and realise that the anxiety has gone. Then come back to now and see how it has changed.

Man is not worried by real problems so much as by his imagined anxieties about real problems.

Epictetus

January 4

Failure

The way we talk to our children becomes their inner voice.

Peggy O'Mara

When you get exhausted, frustrated, overwhelmed or rundown, your body is saying that you are doing things that are none of your business. God does not require of you what is beyond your ability, what leads you away from God, or what makes you depressed or sad.

Henri J M Nouwen

We try so hard.

We try, and we fail. Yet again. And we hate ourselves a little bit more. We don't even have the energy to spiral down the plughole. We lean over and belly-flop into the morass below.

And when we feel like that, we dredge up all the inadequacies we have accumulated since birth.

From the moment we were born, we were told what we should not do. If we were lucky, we may have been told how good we were, too. But we remember those times less well because the pain of criticism did not accompany them.

So here we are now, with this enormous trunk filled with blame, failure and criticism. And it seizes every opportunity it has to slash you with the pain again.

Realise that the things you did were what you needed to do to learn how to live in this world.

Thank yourself for the courage and the strength you have had that has got you this far.

Allow yourself to learn how to live.

Allow yourself to make mistakes.

Your pain is deep, and it won't just go away. It is also uniquely yours, because it is linked to some of your earliest life experiences.

Henri J M Nouwen

January 5

Living

That was the thing about the world: it wasn't that things were harder than you thought they were going to be, it was that they were hard in ways that you didn't expect.

Lev Grossman

Change. Now you see it. Now you don't. It's that quick.

But where is your focus? What are your expectations?

Do you lean toward expecting good outcomes and a promising future, or are you fearing? Are you allowing fear and dis-ease to direct your thinking?

You might call it being uneasy, but I refer to it as dis-ease because that's where it leads to - disease.

Change is the only certainty in life. Everything will change. The greatest pain will cease. The incredible joy will pass. But we can choose our focus. We can direct our thinking.

We can have peace and comfort as long as we live in the present, not in the future or the past.

I'm not in this world to live up to your expectations, and you're not in this world to live up to mine.

Bruce Lee

January 6

Being

If you get tired, learn to rest, not to quit.

Banksy

You do not need to be perfect. Neither do I. Showing up and doing is what we want to do.

Sometimes, even waking up and going back to sleep is the thing we want to do. And sometimes that is the right thing to do.

So many of us waste vast amounts of energy beating ourselves up for what we perceive to be failures and shortcomings – and even resent what we achieve.

Let's give ourselves a break. Let's pat ourselves on the back.

Now.

Do it now.

You are here. Despite everything, you've made it this far. Be proud of that. Love yourself. Allow yourself the freedom to be.

There is virtue in work, and there is virtue in rest. Use both and overlook neither.

Alan Cohen

January 7

Emotions

We cannot selectively numb emotions. When we numb the painful emotions, we also numb the positive emotions.

Brené Brown

And so we withdraw.
We hide.
We deny our positive emotions. We cover our love and joy with the same dank blanket we pull over our negative emotions. We deny our life the ability to live.

Throw yourself entirely into your positive emotions. Embrace them. Share your love and amazement with life.

When you do this, you become able to release your negative emotions. They diminish all on their own. They are so powerful at the moment because by denying them, you are focusing on them.

Let go. Embrace love. Enjoy living.

Your emotions are the slaves to your thoughts, and you are the slave to your emotions.

Elizabeth Gilbert

January 8

Being

When you are guilty, it is not your sins you hate, but yourself.

Anthony de Mello

People (possibly even you) say things like, "I'm depressed." "I'm anxious." "I'm frightened." "I'm lonely."

And, of course, none of these statements are true.

You may be experiencing anxiety, fear or depression, but you are not depression or anxiety or fear. You are greater than that.

If you step outside yourself and observe yourself as if you were looking at someone else, you will see yourself. You will not see depression. You may see someone who is experiencing depression, but you know that they are not depression.

So step out of yourself, step out of anxiety, and see what you can do. You are not trapped. You have a choice.

I prefer to stay alive and be criticized than be sympathized.

Golda Meir

January 9

Ego

*To some people the ego is evil. It gives you so much. It gives
you everything you want. But it takes back too much in
return. It gives you everything; money, riches, women,
glamour, everything you want. But in return, it takes back
so much, and you're soulless. That's its goal. The ego's goal
is to leave you soulless.*

Mike Tyson

From an early age, many of us were taught to cultivate a
strong sense of self-assurance, to take control of our lives,
and to influence others to fulfil our desires and needs.

We were warned that without such assertiveness, we
would be vulnerable to exploitation and failure.

While there may be some truth to this notion, our ego
often becomes a source of external and internal conflict. It
shapes a world according to its desires, disregarding the
suffering of others and even our own.

The ego thrives on our self-doubt and negative emotions,
actively working against our success and happiness.

In this book, when we refer to the ego, we mean the
destructive force within us, the critical voice that
undermines our confidence and sabotages our well-being.

We propose methods to cultivate inner harmony, free
from the destructive influence of the ego.

*Fear seems to have many causes. Fear of loss, fear of
failure, fear of being hurt and so on, but ultimately all fear
is the ego's fear of death, of annihilation. To the ego death is
always just around the corner. In this mind-identified, state
fear of death affects every aspect of your life.*

Eckhart Tolle

January 10

Self-Love

*Every one of us needs to show how much we care for each
other and, in the process, care for ourselves.*

Diana, Princess of Wales

*Low self-esteem is like driving through life with your hand
brake on.*

Maxwell Maltz

Positioning oneself in the perfect place, looking fabulous, and taking a selfie are not forms of self-love.

Self-love is being at peace with oneself and accepting who we are physically, mentally and spiritually.

Self-love and self-forgiveness go hand in hand.

Forgiving others is essential if we are to forgive ourselves.

We cannot love ourselves if we carry a cart full of negative emotions toward others and ourselves.

Self-love is treating the world and ourselves with acceptance, kindness and love. It is freedom.

True friends don't come with conditions.

Aaron Lauritsen

*If you don't love yourself, nobody will. Not only that, you
won't be good at loving anyone else. Loving starts with the
self.*

Wayne Dyer

January 11

Judgement

Be who you are and say what you feel, because those who mind don't matter, and those who matter don't mind.

Bernard M Baruch

That's okay, except when the person judging us is ourselves.

What impossible heights we set ourselves to achieve. Or perhaps our expectations of our capabilities are so low that we do not consider ourselves worthy of the time of day.

Of course, with either of those comes a wave of feelings that overwhelm us as we fight with them. It is so easy to fall into the trap of thinking, "I'm full of fear, hatred, anger, incompetence, uselessness, or all of them!"

When you think about those things, and any others you have chosen to add, you will realise that they are all feelings. These are just feelings that you use to beat yourself up.

This is the truth. A feeling does not define who you are, it is just a feeling, it is you that gives the feeling the meaning it has to you. We have the power to decide how we feel about ourselves, others and situations.

Our feelings do not define us. Who we are is far greater than any passing feeling. Who we are resides quietly, in light, inside us.

When we go there, we find ourselves. The feelings are irrelevant. We can look at the situation and make decisions that are not based on feelings.

Follow your heart, listen to your inner voice, stop caring about what others think.

Roy T Bennett

Be yourself; everyone else is already taken

Oscar Wilde

January 12

<h1 style="text-align:center">Relaxing</h1>

The time to relax is when you don't have time for it.

Sydney J Harris

Learn how to relax, how to just be, soaking up the moment.

Go somewhere where you can stop.

Stop and envelope yourself in your surroundings. Breathe. Look. Take in. Become part of the world you are in. Observe.

Slow everything down.

Slow down even further.

Enjoy.

Take in gently – how you feel.

Make relaxing a part of your daily routine.

Be aware when you are doing it.

Carry its benefits into the rest of your day.

We will be more successful in all our endeavours if we can let go of the habit of running all the time and take little pauses to relax and re-centre ourselves. And we'll also have a lot more joy in living.

Thich Nhat Hanh

January 13

God

You never ask questions when God's on your side.

Bob Dylan

I am watching a women's quarter-final tennis match in one of the Grand Slams.

Both of the players had crucifixes around their necks.

Both of them touched their crucifix in their own way before every point.

One can only assume that they were praying or doing it because they believed that it would increase their chances of winning the point.

It occurs to me that this puts God in a tough spot. What does God do? Does he flip a coin? Does he sit back and watch with enjoyment, one would hope? Does he care at all about who wins? Does he choose the Godliest? Come to that, is he even aware of the event?

Perhaps we should not pray for anything specific – nothing we can put into words – not for ourselves, anyone else, or any group.

Perhaps we should only pray for oneness with God – probably not even with words, but by going into the God inside us and handing everything over to him/her/it.

These are just thoughts, just a way to examine the use of prayer and God. I would never suggest that what you or anyone else is doing is wrong, especially not if it is working.

One of the bravest and toughest things is to let go of that which you cannot control. The only thing you can control is how gracefully you let go.

Lori Schaefer

January 14

Peace

Peace is letting it be. Letting life flow, letting emotions flow through you.

Kamal Ravikant

Do you have peace of mind?
Peace of mind wants to be our goal in life.
With it, anything becomes possible. The route to peace of mind is letting go and forgiveness.
Without doing that, true peace of mind is impossible.
So start.
Start to let go.
Let go of others and yourself.
Forgive.
Forgive others.
Forgive yourself.

Make your heart like a lake, with a calm still surface, and great depths of kindness.

Lao Tzu

January 15

Fear

Fear is only as deep as the mind allows.

Japanese Proverb

Going under the knife.

What a frightening statement. It takes one totally into the horror of an operation over which we have no control.

And when the person it is happening to is someone we love, really love, it is so easy to get stuck in that image of it. Everything is in slow motion. We, they, all stuck as we imagine the knife...

So don't let's do that. Let's travel forward in time to when they will be with us again, exchanging joy and happiness.

Let's find joy.

Wherever you go, go with all your heart.

Confucius

January 16

Frustration

Expectation is the mother of all frustration.

Antonio Banderas

When my son was young, he called the game "Frustration" – <u>Frusastration</u>, and somehow, <u>Frusastration</u> seems to add meaning to the word for me.

I just had a parcel <u>un</u>delivered for about the sixth time, although I made a special effort to be in, and the driver claimed he had delivered it. Bah.

Not to mention all those phone calls. "You are in a queue." "Your call is important to us." "There are sixteen callers in front of you!"

Ah, well, it was only a parcel. I've lived for years and years without it, so I shall manage a few more, I'm sure.

It's important to recognise the <u>frusastration</u> for what it is as soon as it rises through the body and decide not to accept it. To let it go. It is not worth getting aggravated over.

The danger comes when we don't realise it. Then the poison screams around our whole body, roaring with laughter as it goes.

It's the little things that peck at our ankles that do us down if we are not wary.

I've come to believe that all. My past failure and frustration were actually laying the foundation for the understandings that have created the new level of living I now enjoy.

Tony Robbins

January 17

Peace

Choosing stillness in the midst of chaos is the path toward living in peace.

Deepak Chopra

Today, I choose peace.
Perhaps today is too big.
So, I choose peace now, with the plan to keep it in my life.
As I write this, my dog finds her favourite squeaky rubber toy and starts to charge around the room, squeaking loudly. It is the sort of noise that spears its way into your head through the soft spots near your ear.
I choose peace, I reaffirm.
I take a breath. Long and slow.
I choose peace.
And she drops her squeaky toy and lies down, looking out the window.
Choose peace.

You are sky. Everything else is just the weather.

Pema Chodron

There is peace even in the storm.

Vincent van Gogh

January 18

Expectations

Thoughts don't become things; thoughts ARE things.

Eric Micha'el Leventhal

I hope your day is better than you expect.
And what would that be like?
If you knew?
We often go through our days with little expectation or at least little visualised expectation.
If, before the day unfolds, we spend time going through it, painting it how we would like it to be, it is more likely to manifest that way.
Not much of an effort for vast rewards.

The universe is not outside of you. Look inside yourself; everything that you want, you already are.

Rumi

January 19

Ego

I think we all carry the seeds of our own destruction. You really have to be aware that just because something is good, it doesn't mean it's not going to trigger a self-destructive impulse.

Adam Ferrara

The idea that our ego is not our friend is new to many of us when suggested. Surely, it is only looking out for us. Doing its best for us.

But as we delve deeper into the idea and discover the sanity and gentle helping hand of the other voice, our inner voice, we realise that the ego's demands are not helpful.

Yes, with the ego, we may have a few victories. But at what cost?

The ego, our ego, is not our ally. It wants world supremacy at the cost of everyone, including us and our destruction.

Cultivate and strengthen your bond with your gentle, loving inner voice.

Ego is one of the biggest weapons that is used to take us down. It's self-destructive. It's a problem on all levels – even regular people can have big ego problems.

Yehuda Berg

One may understand the cosmos, but never the ego; the self is more distant than any star.

G K Chesterton

January 20

Slowing down

Normal is nothing more than a cycle on a washing machine.

Whoopi Goldberg

Sometimes, rarely, but occasionally, my head, my mind, and my being are in such a state of turmoil that I cannot think straight.

I have heard it described as a washing machine head, though I think that somewhat understates how my mind can cavort. It is intolerable. There used to be nothing I could do about it.

Running with my head down into a supporting wall seemed like a fairly reasonable solution.

Now, I've learned something that works.

So, what do I do when I am experiencing mental pandemonium?

Simple. I say "Slow down" and then "Slow right down".

It is strange how this affects me. All my thoughts slow down, and I can feel the first glimmerings of peace.

"Now stop."

And then, I can choose just one thing to consider calmly and rationally.

Peace.

However, being human, I frequently forget to do this until I am wallowing in the pain intensely.

I'd like to point out that I do not believe we have to suffer!

Things which matter most must never be at the mercy of things which matter least.

Goethe

January 21

Habits

We first make our habits, and then our habits make us.

John Dryden

Choose wisely.

We are not locked into our habits, not totally locked. But prising ourselves away from them is hard. Hard, hard work. Unyielding dedication.

Nonetheless, it is worth the effort if we have habits we would like to discard.

We will never do it in secret. The only way to succeed is to tell others what we are doing. If we try to do it secretly, we give our ego the key to abandoning the struggle.

We also need to choose a new habit that will replace the old one, or we are doomed to failure.

So choose, change, share and enjoy.

Correcting bad habits cannot be done by forbidding or punishment.

Robert Baden-Powell

The only proper way to eliminate bad habits is to replace them with good ones.

Jerome Hines

January 22

Love

What you give today you get tomorrow.

Matshona Dhliwayo

When we view the world with love, the world loves us back.

When we have love and harmony, allow ourselves to love ourselves, and fill ourselves with love, that is what we take with us and spread out into the world.

What we give, we receive.

If our lives, at the moment, are not as good as we would like, the reason, almost certainly, is that we are not pouring enough love into the world.

As we give, we receive.

As we give, so do we receive.

Pure love is a willingness to give without a thought of receiving anything in return.

Peace Pilgrim

January 23

Letting Go

Some of us think holding on makes us strong, but sometimes it is letting go.

Hermann Hesse

We spend so much of our lives trying to control things.
So here is a challenge, a suggestion if you like.
Spend the next few days letting go and letting things just happen.
Relax when you feel yourself tensing up and trust that things will be okay.
And as you do that, "notice" how often things work out without your interference.
At the end of the few days, when you are still here(!), notice the change that has happened within you.
Take it easy.
Be fun to be around.

When the heart truly understands, it lets go of everything.

Ajahn Chah

January 24

Worry

*Once you start worrying, you can worry about anyone,
can't you?*

John Irving

How easily worry entices us into its web, quietly smothering us with one new thread after another.

And how helpless we used to be in its tendrils.

However, we know it only exists because we are thinking about the past, which has gone, and we can do nothing about it.

Or we are trying to predict and create a future which hasn't arrived, and we will not be able to do anything about it until we are there.

So, now, we can move into the present, into this moment, and there are no worries.

There is peace. We can go into our hearts and think from there. And then, as we are confronted with challenges, we can face them with calm stillness.

*Worry does not empty tomorrow of its sorrow, it empties
today of its strength.*

Corrie Ten Boom

January 25

Goodbyes

She laughed when I tried to tell her –
Hello only ends in goodbye.

Rodriguez

I had never thought of that. Hello only ends in goodbye. But it is true. That is obvious.

And somehow, that alters everything. Alters every relationship.

Realising that they will all end in goodbye.

It makes them more precious. It prepares me for goodbye.

It stops me from wanting to cling to things and people as I hope and imagine forever.

It is so freeing.

If you're brave enough to say goodbye, life will reward you with a new hello.

Paulo Coelho

January 26

Respect

As we express our gratitude, we must never forget that the highest appreciation is not to utter words, but to live by them.

John F Kennedy

Reading that quote, the words "but to live by them" leapt out at me.

Because they apply not only to gratitude but also to every area of our lives.

If we are to live in harmony with the world, and particularly with those we live with, then how we LIVE is vital.

If we are not contributing and not committing to the life we live in and with, then we are failing.

If we say, "Yes, I will do that" – and then we don't, we are just blowing raspberries at them.

And for that matter, if we are not doing the necessary things, whether we are asked to or not.

Have respect. Have self-respect. Live as you know you should, whether you're being asked to or not.

Respect yourself and others will respect you.

Confucius

I cannot conceive of a greater loss than the loss of one's self-respect.

Mahatma Gandhi

January 27

Change

A wise man changes his mind, a fool never will.

Icelandic proverb.

Let's be honest. Most of us do not want to change. The very idea of making an effort to change is, well, we think it's an effort...

We often do want things to be different, though. And, of course, that would be so easily accomplished if only they would...

One can almost hear the ego rubbing its hands with glee at the prospect of changing other people.

Or if that isn't on the cards, settling in for those arrows of self-pity and personal futility.

Oddly, we can enjoy instant change by moving our thoughts and behaviours from ourselves and our ego into the peace of our hearts and love.

Change before you have to.

Jack Welch

January 28

Knowing

Knowing others is wisdom. Knowing yourself is enlightenment.

Lao Tzu

I'm going to ask you a question.

The answer is not something you do with words. It is something you feel within your body.

It is about you.

Not anyone else.

Ready?

Here goes...

What does it mean? What does it feel like to be sober?

When you have that, remember it.

Live like that often.

It is different.

It is powerful.

It is freedom,

It is enlightened.

Not creating delusions is enlightenment

Bodhidharma

I believe enlightenment or revelation comes in daily life. I look for joy, the peace of action.

Paulo Coelho

January 29

Freedom

Conformity is the jailer of freedom and the enemy of growth.

John F Kennedy

If liberty means anything at all, it means the right to tell people what they do not want to hear.

George Orwell

There's always another way to do something. If you dare to look.

We easily get stuck in how we do things, how we perceive things, and our certainty that we know how things should be done.

We also get stuck believing there is no way out for us. We simply have to do what is expected of us. The expectation comes from others and also from ourselves.

We are locked in, and the keys have long since been lost. We may even have abandoned the idea that things could or might be different.

But they can be.

It takes courage.

It takes soul searching.

And most importantly, it takes resolve.

They are there if we stop for long enough to go inside ourselves and search for solutions.

Stop being a slave to yourself and others. Decide to walk with freedom.

The view is magical.

Just living is not enough, one must have sunshine, freedom and a little flower.

Hans Christian Andersen

January 30

Blame

There is an expiry date on blaming your parents for steering you in the wrong direction, the moment you are old enough to take the wheel, responsibility lies with you.

J K Rowling

Stop blaming other people and circumstances for killing your dreams. The truth is, we tend to talk ourselves out of acting upon our dreams.

Steve Maraboli

Ah yes, blame…
It's so easy to saunter down that road.
It's so easy to find our "It's because…" to point our finger at.
Even when we know it is not true.
If we do not know that the only person we can blame is ourselves, then it is time to grasp this fact, accept it, and do something about it.
Oh, and no, you are not too old.
Too lazy, perhaps – that hurts, and we should be grateful for the pain.
Perhaps if we intensify the pain enough, we may actually change something.

An irresponsible person is a person who makes vague promises, then breaks his word, blames it on circumstances and expects other people to forgive it.

Ayn Rand

Never blame anyone in your life. Good people give you happiness. Bad people give you experience. Worst people give you a lesson. And the best people give you memories.

Zig Ziglar

January 31

Connection

*When people go within and connect with themselves, they
realise they are connected to the universe, and they are
connected to all living things.*

Armand DiMele

I am here.
You are there.
We are connected.
Our lives brush up against so many people, far more than
we can imagine. Every interaction we have with someone
creates a ripple.
Every act we do impacts the whole.
Even if we were to withdraw and live halfway up a
mountain, we would be changing things. Our not doing or
not interacting with others alters things elsewhere.
So we are needed precisely where we are, talking or not
talking to other people. If we weren't, when we got to the end
of our jigsaw, a piece would be missing, which is impossible.
So whatever is going on in our lives is meant to be and is
essential. We will be involved in it and move to the next
thing and the one beyond.
And so, knowing this, we can, if we choose, feel a certain
peace about what is happening now. Whatever it is.

*The life I touch for good or ill will touch another life, and
that in turn another, until who knows where the trembling
stops or in what far place and time my touch will be felt.
Our lives are linked together. No man is an island.*

Frederick Buechner

Your
thoughts
create
Your
reality

February 1

Perception

It is not that the bee hovers in the seemingly effortless way that it does that amazes me. Rather, it's more the amount of air that it has to move in order to do that.

Craig D Lounsbrough

I watched a mother duck leading its nearly grown ducklings across the water. They seemed to glide effortlessly, magically propelling across the river, turning here and there with no indication of how they were achieving this.

We know how they do it, but even so, it's hard to believe they could be doing anything themselves to accomplish it.

And isn't that how we perceive other humans a lot of the time?

They travel through their day, and we do not give a thought to the inner turmoil that is whizzing around in their heads.

Occasionally, they allow us a look inside, and it overwhelms us. How can they be coping with all that?

And there is, more often than not, very little we can do except to give them love, compassion and the bits of understanding we possess.

What is coming is better than what has gone. Let this belief aim you in the direction you need to go.

Karen Salmansohn

February 2

<h1 style="text-align: center;">Rules</h1>

There are only two lasting bequests we can hope to give our children. One of these is roots, the other wings.

Johann Wolfgang von Goethe

Our parents, the grown-ups in our lives, bind us. When we are young, they throw out their codes of behaviour and ways of thinking and knot them around us. Many of them have come from the generations before and have been passed on unquestioningly.

It is time to sever the ropes and discard the petty rules restricting us.

Choose the rules that serve you in this day and age. Discard the ones holding you back, filling you with low self-worth, when you fail to live up to the false ideals that have been created.

Choose to live.

Choose Freedom. Wisely.

It is easier to build strong children than to repair broken men.

Frederick Douglass

Don't worry that children never listen to you; worry that they are always watching you.

Robert Fulghum

They fuck you up, your mum and dad.
They may not mean to, but they do.
They fill you with the faults they had
And add some extra, just for you.

Philip Larkin

February 3

Pain

Come, Mothers and Fathers
Throughout the land
And don't criticise
What you can't understand.

Bob Dylan

A friend of mine, whose daughter was bullied at school yesterday, has just texted to say that her daughter won't get dressed this morning.

What a mass of emotions this creates when one hears it.

What do you do? Does one bully the daughter into getting dressed?

Somehow, to add bullying to bullying doesn't make sense.

Talk and love are surely the answer, but what energy and commitment they take.

And what? When we, in our own way, in our daily life, are the bullied daughter, dragging ourselves out of bed to return to the obnoxious.

Usually, because it is what we "have to do", we pull on our clothes, mentally and physically, and return, eyes downcast, to the abuse.

Have courage.

As we know, from pain comes growth.

When we have had enough pain, we will change.

Your old road is rapidly agin'.
Please get out of the new one
If you can't lend your hand
For times they are a-changin'.

Bob Dylan

February 4

Patience

It is easier to find men who will volunteer to die, than to find those who are willing to endure pain with patience.

Julius Caesar

Patience was such a foreign notion to me. I demanded instant gratification for myself and from everyone.

And so I led a life of disappointment.

It seems that today, so many people demand instant gratification in so many areas of their lives.

I feel truly blessed that by learning to let go, with the help of friends and meditation, I now enjoy a lot of gentle, comfortable patience.

Perhaps the fact that I believe everything is happening for a reason makes it easier for me to ride the wave of life I am experiencing with grace.

And it is so much more comfortable.

Patience and perseverance have a magical effect before which difficulties disappear and obstacles vanish.

John Quincy Adams

February 5

Time

*Everything that happens in your life and mine, happens
only when the time is right.*

Karen Casey

Accepting that, believing things only happen at the right time, changes them. They do not happen five minutes earlier or five days later. They happen at the right time.

Obviously, we still need to do what we want to prepare for their happening.

We will not win a swimming race if we sit watching TV, eat doughnuts, and never do any exercise. The time to win a swimming race will never arrive.

But the right things will all happen at the right time. No sooner, no later.

So we can stop beating ourselves up about it.

*It's no good going back to yesterday, because I was a
different person then.*

Lewis Carroll – Alice in Wonderland

Kindness

Be kind whenever possible. It is always possible.

Dalai Lama

There.
Be kind.
Throw away your grumpy shoes. Leave them to gather dust. You don't want them anymore.
Take a deep breath.
Fill yourself with kindness.
(Yes, even the little bit you're hiding)
Fill yourself full of kindness and gratitude.
And go forth spreading it.
Enjoy.
There is magic there.
Real magic.
Grasp it.
Enjoy.

How do we change the world? One random act of kindness at a time.

Morgan Freeman

February 7

Shame

Shame is among the most powerful and destructive of human emotions.

Soroosh Shahrivar

"Shame."
"What a shame."
"I'm so ashamed."
"Shame on you!"
"I can never go back there or see them again!"
Shame – what a killer. What a soul wrecker, a poisonous word and feeling.

How dreadful. How humiliating. How disgusting.

Let's forbid "shame" in our lives.

If someone is shaming you in any way, reject it. Ask them, "Do you want to make me feel ashamed?"

Say, "Do you know that shame poisons the blood of both the giver and the receiver?"

Say, "I do not want to swim with anyone who bathes with shame."

Discard it.

Refuse to be around it.

Exist with pride.

Shame is the silent killer of potential.

Dana L Stringer

February 8

What if

You'll never get anywhere if you go about what-iffing like that.

Roald Dahl

What if?

If, buts and maybes?

Ah, yes, what a wonderful source of inner turmoil. What a destroyer of sanity.

What if this happens? Or doesn't happen. Or if she does, or if he doesn't...

Spinning out of control. Giving control to others or the world. Giving up control because we can no longer think clearly.

Somewhere in there is a clue. We don't have control over others. They do, or they don't, and we want to realise that, accept it and stop fretting.

There is another clue, too. If we are "what-iffing", we are not in the present. And the present is where calm and peace exist. Nowhere else.

So if you find a "What-if" poking its head into your mind, realise this is a sign that you are not in the present.

What if there was no tomorrow, and everyone showed up anyway...

Nanette L Avery

February 9

Being

The only journey is the one within.

Rainer Maria Rilke

At the very heart of me, at the deepest part of me, I know who I am.

Bethany Auriel-Hagan

We forget.
We forget to look.
We do not look.
We do not know.
The storms and noise of life engulf us, and we fight mindlessly. We ignore the idea that we could surrender.

And yet, I would like to remind you and myself that however unspeakably horrible things may be, there is peace and answers inside our being.

We do not have to go on being locked into whatever behaviour or self-torture we are experiencing.

We have a choice.
If we claim it.

The most important thing is to enjoy your life – to be happy – it's all that matters.

Steve Jobs

February 10

Difference

I see the human race at the mouth of a long dark tunnel, and right at the end of that tunnel is a little star, and that's hope. But we don't just sit at the mouth of the tunnel and hope that that star will come to illuminate us. We have to crawl under, climb over, work our way around all the obstacles that lie between us and hope.

Dame Jane Goodall

Are we doing our bit?

Are you, am I, doing our bit to help make the changes we need to reach the star that is hope?

What can you do today to inch towards it? Tomorrow may be too late.

We need to consciously do something today that will make a difference.

The greatest threat to our planet is the belief that someone else will save it.

Robert Swan

February 11

Focus

We choose our joys and sorrows long before we experience them.

Kahlil Gibran

When we focus on what we lack, we create lack and misery in our lives.

We create not having, even never having. The idea of having is an unseen shadow that hides in the dark corners, never to be revealed.

If we want, if we desire abundance and plenty, we want to change our focus. Change our mindset from one of lack to one of gratitude for all the things in our lives.

Focusing on gratitude and feeling gratitude in our bodies starts the flow of plenty and even more into our lives.

Embrace gratitude.

Trust in dreams, for in them is hidden the gate to eternity.

Kahlil Gibran

February 12

Letting Go

A man needs a little madness, or else... he never dares cut the rope and be free.

Nikos Kazantzakis

So many people spend their lives clinging to doing the "right" thing, not wanting to be noticed.

When things go wrong, they scream and text about all the injustices they perceive, never daring to be human beings, never allowing themselves out of the cage they have so carefully created.

They look out and blame, blame and wail, refusing to let go of the injustices, blind to their part in any of it.

Their road to freedom could be achieved by realising their part and letting go of the blame, the anger, the finger-pointing.

It takes two to tango, but just one dance with the devil and to bring the house down.

Jason Versey

February 13

Forgiveness

Forgiveness is for you – not the other person. It's something you do inside yourself that you feel in your body and heart that releases you from your past and frees you to live life fully.

Barbara J Hunt

I met a friend who'd just seen his father for the first time in thirteen years. He went to tell his dad that he was sorry.

"What did you do wrong?" I asked.

"Very little. He was a violent, angry and unpleasant man, but I needed to apologise to him for my peace of mind. Even if, in truth, my only crime had been being there."

"And how did it go?"

"Really well, he was old and shrivelled, no longer terrifying. I felt sorry for him. He didn't say he was sorry for what he'd done. I don't think it even occurred to him that he had ever done anything wrong. But we parted as human beings... I shan't see him again."

We want to forgive the world and everyone in it. Without forgiveness, we deny ourselves peace.

Oh, and most importantly, we want to forgive ourselves. If we do not forgive ourselves, we can never know peace.

Today, I decided to forgive you. Not because you apologised, or because you acknowledged the pain that you caused me, but because my soul deserves peace.

Najwa Zebian

We are not perfect, forgive others as you want to be forgiven.

Catherine Pulsifer

February 14

Reacting

One bad turn does not excuse another.

Richelle E Goodrich

As children, we learn to retaliate – to attack to get what we want. We may use other tactics, too, but the negative behaviour tends to produce what we want quickly, so we use that.

We may switch to loving behaviour to achieve what we want, but that is not really loving. It is just a more subtle form of manipulation.

And so it goes, until now. Here we are, almost certainly using the same tactics, and if we no longer are, we know people who are.

When people do something we don't like, our knee-jerk reaction is to attack them or withdraw our love and support. "See how they get on without my help, love, and support!"

Even though we know by now that everything that is not love is a cry for help.

And that being the case, what can we do to change the situation?

Withholding love is a form of self-sabotage, as what we withhold from others, we are withholding from ourselves.

Marianne Williamson

February 15

Trees

Trees are poems that the earth writes upon the sky.

Kahil Gibran

When did you last lie under a tree and look at the light shining through the leaves?

When did you last lie under a tree and envelope yourself in the wonder and light of the sunshine (if there is any) flashing into your being?

When did you last stop long enough to connect with peace?

When will you next lie beneath a tree and let all the light flow into you and the earth draw all the unwanted darkness from your body?

When?

"Listen to the trees talking in their sleep," she whispered as he lifted her to the ground. "What nice dreams they must have!"

L M Montgomery

February 16

Blame

I am not what happened to me. I am what I choose to become.

Carl Jung

It is so easy to blame one's past for one's present. So easy to find reasons why we missed out because... or to be locked into our view of the world because...

And yet, for most of us, there are moments when we discard all of that and rise, becoming the competent and magnificent person we are capable of being.

And if we can do that, even if only for a few seconds, then we can do it. We do not have to go through our lives crushed by the burden of the past.

We can choose who we want to be and then be that person, even if we keep re-enacting our old beliefs and behaviours.

You can get discouraged many times, but you are not a failure until you begin to blame someone else and stop trying.

John Burroughs

February 17

Change

You cannot escape the responsibility of tomorrow by evading it today.

Abraham Lincoln

I might not have noticed if it had only happened once, but twice, almost on top of one another.

I have two friends who have both recently given up therapy. They said to me in different ways that they did not like what was happening to them. It was too much to cope with... perhaps they'd go back later...

And I realised that it was their ego talking. Things were happening that their ego could not control. It hated it. It deluged them with pain to ensure that it could keep them under control.

Of course, we don't need to go through therapy for this to happen. Our ego will find ways to attack us whenever we embark on change.

So perhaps, by realising this, we can make the changes we want in our lives and ourselves. We are refusing to allow our ego to dominate us.

Desperation is the raw material of drastic change. Only those who can leave behind everything they have ever believed in can hope to escape.

William S Burroughs

February 18

Loneliness

People think being alone makes you lonely, but I don't think that's true. Being surrounded by the wrong people is the loneliest thing in the world.

Kim Culbertson

Sometimes we feel lonely.

It creeps gently into us in the same way that darkness fills the room at dusk, imperceptibly stealing the light.

And more often than not, it just flows on and away, almost unnoticed.

But there are times when its grasp, and the pain that comes with it, is much stronger. Our natural reaction is to withdraw, to curl up in a ball as the kicks pound into us.

The cure, the solution, is, of course, action. Just moving our body will start to change the way we feel.

Then, call someone, go out, talk to people in the supermarket queue, and get involved in the world.

After all, what is the worst that loneliness can do? No more than we allow it to.

It's better to be unhappy alone than unhappy with someone – so far.

Marilyn Monroe

February 19

Love

Beauty is eternity gazing at itself in a mirror.

Kahlil Gibran

*Look at yourself in the mirror, and don't be afraid to notice
how beautiful you are.*

Yoko Ono

Smile at yourself in your bathroom mirror.
Smile. Say, "Good morning".
Look at yourself. Smile some more. Say, "I love you".
So often, we look at ourselves without looking. Without
noticing. Without focusing. Without any love.
Wink at yourself. It's fun.
Look at yourself. Smile. Say, "I love you".
Everyday.
Notice the difference.
Do it every day for the rest of your life.
Be kind to yourself.
Be joyous.

*Smile in the mirror. Do that every morning and you'll start
to see a big difference in your life.*

Yoko Ono

Thoughts

If you realised how powerful your thoughts are, you would never think a negative thought.

Peace Pilgrim

Your thoughts create your day.
Your thoughts create your perceptions.
Your perceptions are what make the day the way it is.
Your thoughts create your day.

If you want a good day, start the day with positive thoughts, words, and expectations.

The first thing I say aloud when I wake up is, "Thank you, thank you, thank you, God, for my sleep and my dreams. God, give me a sober day today. Help me to achieve whatever miracles you want of me. Help me to see things differently."

I smile. I travel through my day in my head, imagining that each event that I know about will happen and end well.

I don't "go into the event", I go beyond it, and visualise it having gone well for the good of all the people concerned.

I travel to the end of my day and see myself going to bed, the day having gone well.

At the end of my day, the last thing I say aloud is, "Thank you, thank you, thank you." It takes no time. It makes a vast difference. I know because on the rare occasions I have not done it, my day has been less than good.

When a flower doesn't bloom, you fix the environment in which it grows, not the flower.

Alexander Den Heijer

February 21

Perception

When we shift our perception, our experience changes.

Lindsay Wagner

When bad things happen, when disaster strikes, when our world is turned upside down, it is hard to believe that it is for our own good. It seems impossible to accept that.

We want to remember that it is our perception of the event that has chosen to see it as a disaster.

And we have control over how we perceive things if we choose to use that control.

By moving our ego's screams aside and listening to our inner voice, we can understand and accept that what has happened or is happening is part of our journey.

It is there so that we can grow and become.

We do not have to choose the negative, horrendous viewpoint. We can breathe in and be, and in so doing, we can change how we deal with it.

We have strength, power, and love.

There is no truth. There is only perception.

Gustave Flaubert

February 22

Happiness

The best way to cheer yourself up is to try to cheer someone else up.

Mark Twain

Most folks are about as happy as they make up their minds to be.

Abraham Lincoln

There you have it. Simple words of wisdom. Easy to do.
All we have to do is do it.
It is our choice.
The benefits to us and the world are incalculable.

There is no path to happiness. Happiness is the path.

Buddha

Habits

I would advise any 17-year-old to surround yourself with people who listen to you, nod when you speak and smile when you enter spaces.

Janet Mock

Are you a head nodder or a shaker?

When you move your head, do you habitually nod or shake it?

Check it out. You probably don't know. But we tend to have one or the other that we do without thinking.

If you discover you are a shaker, I recommend changing and becoming a nodder.

When we nod, we are saying "Yes" to ourselves at an unconscious level. And we can function so much better when we are being positive.

Enjoy.

Against her ankles as she trod,
The lucky buttercups did nod.

Jean Ingelow

February 24

Ego

The solitary ego that revolves around itself, and feeds upon itself, ends up strangled by a great cry or a great laugh.

Stendhal

Let that be a warning to you!
Either learn to control and bypass your ego, or end up choked.
The ego is not your friend.
Do not entertain it.
Refuse to allow it to sit and spout into your brain.
Choose freedom.
Choose love.
Choose peace.

Awareness and ego cannot coexist.

Eckhart Tolle

To feel that life is meaningless unless "I" can be permanent is like having fallen in love with an inch.

Alan Watts

February 25

Choice

Tactics without strategy is the noise before defeat.

Sun Tzu

Start with what is right rather than what is acceptable.

Franz Kafka

It is so easy to go through our life with little thought about the things that are important.

Yes, we think constantly about all manner of things, most of which we have no control over.

Our ego revelling in our discomfort as we rehash one impossible scenario after another.

Let's look at it all for a moment. We know how to have peace by now. How to discard the fear, the blame and the self-abuse.

So we do it. And then immediately, more often than not, we snap back into our bog of pain.

Why?

No, seriously, why?

What sane person would do that?

We have wisdom, knowledge, and gentle understanding that sets us apart from the masses.

So please choose to use it.

Two roads diverged in a wood, and I – I took the one less travelled by, and that has made all the difference.

Robert Frost

February 26

Soul

*Put your heart, mind and soul into even your smallest acts.
This is the secret of success.*

Swami Sivananda

Are you just a body?
Or are you a soul?
Do you have a soul?
Does your soul live inside you?
Oh, and while we are asking, do you have an ego that yaks and rules you day and night?

I have a soul.

Actually, I believe I am a soul in a body.
Whenever I am wise enough to choose, I can talk to my soul and get the advice and guidance I want.
All I have to do is reject the voice of the ego. Switch it off if you like.
There is the wisdom, peace and love of my soul.
So good.

The soul always knows what to do to heal itself. The challenge is to silence the mind.

Caroline Myss.

Let your soul stand cool and composed before a million universes.

Walt Whitman

February 27

Love

*Do your a little bit of good where you are. It is those little
bits of goods put together that overwhelm the world.*

Desmond Tutu

It's a good day to do good.
Do good for others and yourself.
Focus on how you can do things for other people.

How can you be present for them when you are with
them? Focus on what they are saying and how you can
interact positively with them. Give yourself entirely in every
interaction you have.

Doing this is not only good for them, it is good, wonderful
even, for us.

And let us not forget to be good and do good for
ourselves, too. Let us not abuse our bodies and minds with
"stuff" that we know, in our hearts, is not good for us.

Instead, let us pamper ourselves with things that are
mentally and physically uplifting. So much better.

*Everyone has inside of him a piece of good news. The good
news is you don't know how great you can be! How much
you can love! What you can accomplish! And what your
potential is.*

Anne Frank

February 28

Control

*You have power over your mind – not outside events –
realise this, and you'll find strength.*

Marcus Aurelius

We may, we might, if we are diligent, have some control over ourselves.

We certainly have the power to choose what we think when we remember to use that power.

Many never do. They crash through their lives, bouncing from one ego-driven desire to the next.

But leaving all that aside, what is so important to learn, know, acknowledge, and understand is that we do not have control over others.

Yes, they may do what we ask, but only for as long as they want to. Then, they revert to being their own master. (Even if they are not truly their own master, but just their ego's puppet.)

Realising this and accepting that we will never have control of them can be very liberating. If we choose to accept it, we can have a more peaceful life.

To take back your power in any given situation, focus on the things you can control. The thoughts you choose to think is usually the best place to start.

Anthon St Maarten.

February 29

Change

We have nothing that really is our own; we hold everything as a loan.

Nicolas Poussin

There is only one constant in this world, in the universe, and that is change. Everything changes. All the time. Everything begins and ends. Everything.

We so want things to go on.

And they don't.

Ever.

Strangely, when we realise and accept that, everything becomes so much easier.

You may find what you're looking for and realise it is not the answer.

Ahmed Mustafa

Everything is so fleeting and impermanent. It's enough to drive you batshit crazy.

Shane Kuhn

Keep
it
simple

March 1

Choice

*Be miserable. Or motivate yourself. Whatever has to be
done, it's always your choice.*

Wayne Dyer

You are the author of your book, your own life. You
choose where the next mark on the page will be and the one
after that.

Sometimes, you may think you have no choice, but you
do. Even the hunted, the trapped animal, has a choice about
how to react to the next moment, whether to struggle or
capitulate.

We do have choices.

We can choose.

Just because we have done it and reacted a certain way
for many years does not mean we have to do it like that
now. We may choose to, but if we do, we want to recognise
that it is our choice.

We have freedom, even when we do not choose to claim it

*Everything can be taken away from man, but one thing: the
last of the human freedoms – to choose one's attitude in any
given set of circumstances, to choose one's own way.*

Viktor Frankl

Gratitude

Today's tears water tomorrow's gardens.

Matshona Dhliwayo

Gratitude.
Pain.
Suffering.
It's so easy to be happy, yes, yes, yes. Gratitude. It's so easy. It's so very easy.

But hang on a moment. All our growth, learning, change, being and becoming have come from pain and suffering. If we had not had and gone through them, we would not be able to walk.

One step. Fall over. Pain and humiliation. Fuck this. Never walk.

So...

So whatever we are going through, yes, whatever the pain and the suffering, even if it is just our last throws before death, is there for a reason. A learning. As something we can give to others. Even if there is no apparent benefit for us.

So...

So thank it. Feel <u>genuine</u> gratitude for it. <u>Genuine</u> gratitude. Feel it with your body. Your mind will change.

And the pain and the suffering will change, too. The pain and the suffering will change.

It's a lot different to say "thank you" to God instead of asking for stuff. That's the way I used to pray. Help me, God. Do this for me, God. I'm mad at you, God, fix it. I don't pray like that anymore. The only prayer I say now is thank you.

Josie Robinson

March 3

Impatience

What good has impatience ever brought? It has only served as the mother of mistakes and the father of irritation.

Steve Maraboli

Impatience.
Whatever it is, however, we are doing it. It is just impatience. It is the desire to alter the process.
<u>Often</u>, we don't even process it as impatience. We want it now. Or if not now, then very soon.
Or maybe we wanted something to stop yesterday.
We can't wait for the holiday or the other person to do it or be how we want.
There is a time for things. They happen when they happen. If we can allow them and ourselves to move forward, they will.
Impatience wastes our time thinking about things that cannot happen until they do.
Relax. Allow. Enjoy the moment you are in.

The common man prays, "I want a cookie right now!" And God responds, "If you'd listen to what I say, tomorrow it will bring you 100 cookies."

Criss Jami

Me love to eat Cookies. Sometimes eat whole, sometimes me chew it.

Cookie Monster

Help

You are never strong enough that you don't need help.

César Chávez

One of the biggest defects in life is the inability to ask for help.

Robert Kiyosaki

One of the most challenging things we can do or say is. "I can't do this alone. I need help."

And then, of course, accepting the help.

The difficulty many people face is they ask for help and then ignore it or take advantage of it.

So don't be afraid to ask for help, but be mindful when you do, accept it gracefully and do your part wholeheartedly.

Asking for help isn't weak; it's a great example of how to take care of yourself.

Charlie Brown

March 5

Change

Our greatest glory is not in never falling, but in rising every time we fall.

Confucious

And the rain came – big rains, on and on. There was much flooding, and my river was flowing extremely fast.

I watched a pair of swans swimming as fast as they could upstream while they moved slowly backwards – the idea of walking or flying never occurring to them.

And I wondered how often we do that. Struggle on and on, regardless of the fact that we are making no headway, even losing ground. But still, we battle on, resolutely refusing to consider doing things differently.

How sad. How strange. How dreadful.

Perhaps this can be the wake-up call to change how we tackle our challenges.

If we dare?

Everyone thinks of changing the world, but no one thinks of changing himself.

Leo Tolstoy

March 6

Peace

I shall look at you out of the corner of my eye, and you will say nothing. Words are the source of misunderstandings.

Antoine de Saint-Exupéry

In the morning, when I sit by my window, looking out over the river, as I read and meditate, my dog comes and curls up at my feet.

Is it because of the peace I am in?

Then, when I move to this table to sit and write, she often gets up onto my lap. She wants to be involved, poking my pens and paper with her nose.

It seems that we are constantly giving information to the people we are with, whether we are speaking or not.

And so if we approach others with a gentle feeling of love and quiet, they will know at some level and be far more open when we communicate.

The way we communicate with others and with ourselves ultimately determines the quality of our lives.

Tony Robbins

March 7

Forgiveness

*Forgive others, not because they deserve forgiveness, but
because you deserve peace.*

Jonathon Lockwood Huie

Not forgiving is like clasping a burning coal to your chest and wanting the other person, whom you feel hatred towards, to burn.

But you are the one who suffers.

So forgive them.

If you make a mistake, do whatever you can to make amends, and then forgive yourself.

Stop clinging to self-loathing.

Let go.

Live in the peace that forgiveness offers.

*Forgiveness is, above all, a personal choice, a decision of the
heart, to go against the natural instincts to pay back evil
with evil.*

Pope John Paul II

*The weak can never forgive. Forgiveness is an attribute of
the strong.*

Mahatma Gandhi

Rejection

You don't have to disrespect and insult others simply to hold your own ground. If you do, that shows how shaky your own position is.

Red Haircrow

When people disrespect us, abuse, reject, or neglect us, our automatic defence system snaps into action.

It also launches itself when we imagine or expect negative behaviour from others. It doesn't even have to be real other than in our minds.

And so we start to build a prison, brick by brick, to shut out the pain we experience from the world – time after time, surrounding ourselves, imprisoning ourselves in a windowless cell of our own making.

We are the ones who are hurting, damaging, and abusing ourselves.

Push a brick away today. The world will not end. Push away another. Move into the light that exists in the world that is waiting to shine on you.

It is better that way, much nicer!

I freed one thousand slaves; I could have freed a thousand more if only they knew they were slaves.

Harriet Tubman

March 9

Letting Go

I waited for something
And something died.
So I waited for nothing
And nothing arrived.

Villagers – Conor Joseph O'Brien

Oh dear.

So much of our lives are wasted, and we have no idea why. We are just bouncing down a hill like an accidentally dislodged stone. From nowhere, bouncing, and on to a new nowhere.

That's it unless we decide to take charge. How do we take charge? (I'm slightly frightened to say this.) By letting go.

As the tumbling stone, we think we are in control. Go here, go there, bounce over there. But we are not.

The only way we can regain control is by letting go and letting our inner being take charge so we can move through our lives elegantly while benefitting others.

It is so good to no longer be a bouncing stone. So incredibly good. Even if we only achieve it occasionally, it is so much better.

Let others argue over small things, but not you.
Let others cry over small hurts, but not you.
Let others leave their future in someone else's hands,
But not you.

Jim Rohn

March 10

Judgement

People often miss out on their own human genius because they're trying to be more perfect than the gods.

Curtis Tyrone Jones

We were almost certainly weaned on judgement. If we had siblings, we were compared to each other's successes and failures, though obviously, we didn't need siblings for that to happen.

In our household, the way we did things was different, better or worse than how others behaved.

So we were force-fed judgement, and our ego loved it and grew stronger daily.

The root cause of judgement is, of course, fear.

And every time we replace the judgement in our lives with acceptance, so replacing fear with love, the stronger, the more complete we become.

No one is born ugly, we're just born in a judgemental society.

Kim Namjoon

Love

Until we have seen someone's darkness, we don't really know who they are. Until we have forgiven someone's darkness, we don't really know what love is.

Marianne Williamson

Sometimes, our relationship with someone drags us down. We bend over backwards, trying to make it go well. And perhaps we even engage in battle with them. If someone pokes us repeatedly, it hurts, and our instinct is to retaliate. We are human, after all.

However, if we remember that everything is fear or love and everything that is not love is a cry for help, we start to see it differently.

If what they are doing is a cry for help, then we want to shower them with love. Use every opportunity we have to surround them with love. Find loving things to say to them in response to their abuse or complaints.

The love they crave is not material, and they may have to work through that to understand it. But by not rising to their attacks and by being present and filled with love, we will slowly change their behaviour because our response is no longer what they crave.

Accept the children as we accept trees – with gratitude, because they are a blessing – but do not have expectation or desires. You don't expect trees to change, you love them as they are.

Isabel Allende

March 12

Fear

One of the greatest discoveries a man makes, one of his great surprises, is to find he can do what he was afraid he couldn't do.

Henry Ford

Sometimes, we know what we fear, as it consumes us. Sometimes, we have no idea what it is, and we feel the fear wrap around us like a damp mist.

With either, I have found that if I shake myself, like a dog shaking off water, I can rid myself of it.

Most fear is not real. It is just our ego having fun at our expense.

When the thing is happening, we do not fear it. We do it. Fear is anticipation. Fear is unreal. It does not exist. Shake it off.

Live.

Experience.

Enjoy.

The only thing you fear is the unreality that you yourself have invented.

Byron Katie

Remember, sometimes, not getting what you want is a wonderful stroke of luck.

Dalai Lama

Perfection

*Who are you to judge the life I live? I know I'm not perfect –
and I don't live to be – but before you start pointing
fingers... make sure your hands are clean.*

Bob Marley

Hey!
You are not perfect.
You never have been.
Nobody has ever been perfect.
And that is okay.
Yup.
You can take a deep breath, gently sink into your body, and realise you are okay. You are doing alright.

We all have shortcomings or self-doubts in our lives. So, give yourself a break. If you haven't done "this" or "that" perfectly, it does not matter. The world will not end.

Get on with your life. Do what you can. Leave what you can't do undone. Accept yourself.

When you do that, you are more likely to achieve things. You won't have wasted your energy beating yourself up.

*No one is looking at your imperfections; they're all too busy
worrying about their own.*

Isaac Mizrahi

March 14

Change

Everything changes, and somewhere along the line, I'm changing with it.

Eric Burdon

Everything changes.

It is so easy to forget that. To somehow assume that it will go on. To be unable to imagine that it will not go on.

Of course, sometimes we are desperate for things to change, for anything to get us out of this hell. And yet, it seems to go on and on. We give up hope that it will ever alter.

But it will.

Maybe not in the time frame we would like.

Take it all in and accept that change is coming so we can enjoy the good things we are experiencing now.

I'm a Buddhist, so one of my biggest beliefs is, "Everything changes, don't take it personally".

Alan Ball

March 15

Love

You were made perfectly to be loved.

Elizabeth Barrett Browning

We enter a room, a space, a building, the world, and we set, in our mind, how we will be received.
We determine how everything will go before it happens.
Go in believing you are loved.
Believe it.
Spread the idea into the world before you.
It changes everything.
You are loved.
Enjoy!

If you wish to be loved, love.

Seneca

Routines

The secret of your future is hidden in your daily routine.

Mike Murdock

It was Wednesday, so I was taking the bins out. I met a neighbour who was dragging his bins to the street. He was sweating. He stopped and looked at me. "Wonderful Wednesday," he said, "don't you just love it? Bin day. Something that breaks the routine." We chatted for another minute and then dashed in, out of the rain.

"He was joking," I thought. And then I wondered, "Was he joking?" Is this the only break in his routine? Is he trapped in a loop of nothingness, which is only disrupted by taking the bins out?

Most of us probably experience several loops in our day or week. We can find ways to enhance them so they don't trap us.

We can choose to spot freshness in what we are doing, even if it is the twelfth time we have done it this week, or today, or in the last hour.

We are not robots. Let's find the delight in what we do.

You will never change your life until you change something you do daily.

Mike Murdock

No one knows what it's like...
to be a dustbin...
in Shaftesbury...
with hooligans...

Bill Hicks

March 17

Acceptance

One does not discover new lands without consenting to lose sight of the shore for a very long time.

André Gide

When something really bad is going on in a culture, the average guy doesn't see it. He can't. He's average and surrounded by and immersed in the cant and the discourse of the status quo.

George Saunders

We take so many things in our lives for granted. Things are the way they are. It is unimaginable that they could be any other way.

But suppose, just for a moment, how incredibly different your life would be if the South had won the American Civil War. Or if Germany had won World War One. Or if Japan and Germany had won the Second World War.

Everything would be very different.

And yet, we take everything in our lives as just being the way they are.

Strange.

How do we express our gratitude?

Assuming that you were on the winning side.

With success comes complacency if you let it happen. It is human nature; there is that urge to think about how well you have done.

Chris Coleman

March 18

Peace

Peace of mind for five minutes, that's what I crave.

Alanis Morissette

Do you want peace in your life?
Do you have peace in your life?
If not, why not?
You've heard, you know even, that what you give is what you get. What we put out into the world is what we receive back. We may think we want peace, but what are we focussing on, obsessing about, talking and complaining about? Not peace, evidently.

Our old pal, the ego, transmits our agitation, so that is what we get in return: turmoil.

All we have to do to have peace is to step aside from our thoughts, go inside, into the peace, love, and quiet of our inner being and claim that. Go out and give that to the world.

Stop fighting everything. As long as you are fighting, there will never be peace. Yet, it is so close and available to all of us.

It isn't enough to talk about peace. One must believe in it.
And it isn't enough to believe in it. One must work at it.

Eleanor Roosevelt

March 19

Growth

Challenges make you discover things about yourself that you never really knew.

Cicely Tyson

Oh, how we want to protect the ones we love. We wish we could carry their burdens, suffer their pain instead of them, and enable them to be free from fear.

So much fear haunts them. If only we could get them to understand that everything will work out. That today's struggles will be gone.

We cannot do it.

We all have to travel our own road. We can be there for them with love, but we cannot do it for them.

Nor can we protect them. We all grow by travelling through the difficulties that confront us in our lives.

If you never let your child cross the road alone, he is far more likely to get run down later.

Be honest about yourself. Give your love. Give freedom.

Do not demand.

Give love.

Give freedom.

Friendship and selfless support are what matters. These are the priceless blessings in life that help us to overcome every difficult life experience and challenge.

Lily Amis

March 20

Progress

The man who has no imagination has no wings.

Muhammad Ali

You say, "Well, I have an imagination!"

Good, great, but do you use it?

How often do you go to bed feeling that you have reached your potential?

How often do you go to bed knowing you have taken a step, or even half a step, towards achieving one of your goals? And how frequently do you praise yourself and overwhelm yourself with gratitude for your achievements?

The man who views the world the same at fifty as he did at twenty has wasted thirty years of his life.

Muhammed Ali

March 21

God

*The highest form of ignorance is when you reject something
you don't know anything about.*

Wayne Dyer

I was talking to a friend the other day who said she couldn't believe that God had arranged for the experiences that had happened in her life. She didn't think there was a God, and if there was, she couldn't imagine that he knew or cared about her.

And I thought back to my childhood idea of God, the conventional man in the clouds, and I remembered thinking as she did.

The idea of God was created by man for himself to calm his fears. And I cannot tell you how or when my thoughts and beliefs about God changed. It's been a slow, gentle, loving process to the stage where I know that "god" is within me. And I believe God is within you and everyone if we allow ourselves to feel, experience, and be guided by God.

*Good human qualities – honesty – sincerity, a good heart –
cannot be bought with money, nor can they be produced by
machines, but only by the mind itself. We can call this the
inner light or God's blessing, or human quality. This is the
essence of mankind.*

Dalia Lama

Now

All flesh is as grass and all the glory of man is as the flower of grass.

Jaroslav Hašek

What is the year that is most important to you?
The year you were born?
Christ's birth?
1783 Independence Day?
1066 Conquest of England?
2550 BC, the construction of the Pyramids?
Or none of the above?
But whatever it is, the few hundred or thousand years pale into insignificance when you think, for a second or two, that the Earth is 4.5 billion years old.

Our time here is so insignificant. Before you've even started to blink, it has gone.

Absolutely nothing is as significant as we imagine.

Even if it is truly important, in a few years, it and you will be forgotten.

So, give yourself a break and enjoy the tiny flash that is your life.

I am here, and here is nowhere in particular.

William Golding

March 23

Self-belief

One of the great cosmic laws, I think, is that whatever we hold in our thoughts will come true in our experience. When we hold something, anything, in our thoughts, then somehow coincidence leads us in the direction we've been wishing to lead ourselves.

Richard Bach

Yesterday, I went to a Christmas fair with a friend. It wasn't great, so we didn't stay long. Our car was parked on a grass hill amidst a few thousand vehicles, and I could not reverse out of the space – wheels spinning in the thick mud!

My friend went off to find some help to push us out. I stayed and meditated, sending a message to the owner of the red Audi parked in front of us to return to their car.

The pushers arrived unwillingly. "We're not employed to push cars." This was true, obviously they weren't. They couldn't push my car. It just slid sideways towards the car parked on its right.

Then, the owner of the red Audi parked in front arrived, drove off, and we escaped through the gap.

Coincidence?

You may call it a coincidence if you wish. I know that it was not.

Coincidence is God's way of remaining anonymous.

Albert Einstein

In the Hebrew language, there's no such word as coincidence.

Paula White

March 24

Anger

Anger is an acid that can do more harm to the vessel in which it is stored than to anything on which it is poured.

Mark Twain

Before you embark on a journey of revenge, dig two graves.

Confucius

Anger. Self-Pity. Grief. Joy. Elation. Misery. Boredom. Enlightenment.

We do them, or we don't do them, to ourselves.

You cannot make me happy, angry, sad, pathetic, joyful, or enlightened.

I do it to myself.

I choose it.

I increase it and even lose myself in it. You may or may not be doing it with me. If you are, we feed off each other. But still, I am in charge of my feelings.

If I regularly experience feelings that I don't like, I want to change my behaviour.

If I am not meditating and sharing my challenges with someone, then they are unlikely to change or go.

If I remember, every time I do a negative feeling, "I am choosing to do this to myself," I may stop long enough to choose a different feeling.

Holding on to anger is like grasping a hot coal with the intent of throwing it at someone else – you are the one who gets burned.

Buddha

March 25

Happiness

Happiness is a choice, not a result. Nothing will make you happy until you choose to be happy.

Ralph Marston

It's my choice.

I choose how I react to every experience and thought that I have. And it goes through everything I do.

There was a time when I would expect, and dive into, every negative aspect of pretty much anything – if not everything. And my life, if you will excuse my language – was shit.

Somewhere along the line, with the help of AA and meditation, coupled with a massive desire to change, I did.

Everything is fear or love.

Even the most negative things that happen to me have some positive aspects, however hard they may be to uncover.

And now, with sanity and joy in my heart, I keep going until I can find the positive. Then I focus on that.

It is my choice.

I have a choice.

I choose the positive. I like that so much more.

Very little is needed to make a happy life; it is all within yourself, in your way of thinking.

Marcus Aurelius

Inner Voice

You can either be a host to God or a hostage to your ego. It's your call.

Wayne Dyer

Life is so simple. There is only one choice we have to make.

And that is to listen to our inner voice rather than our ego. When we do that, all our challenges evaporate.

Yes, we may still have stuff in our lives that we have to face and deal with. But with our inner voice, our higher self, our soul, and the holy spirit as our ally or guide, we will find the solutions we need.

Listening to our ego has become such a go-to habit that we may find re-tuning to our inner voice difficult. But persevere, the rewards are boundless.

The ego-self constantly pushes reality away. It constructs a future out of empty expectations and a past out of regretful memories.

Alan Watts

A bad day for your ego is a great day for your soul.

Jillian Michaels

March 27

Freedom

... a lie told once is easy to expose, but a lie told a thousand times can look like the truth. And destroy the world.

Mitch Albom

Since birth, we have been programmed by parents, ancestors, teachers, and society. We have been brainwashed with their thoughts, behaviours, and expectations.

We have been lied to, suppressed and forced to fall into line.

This is how things are done. This is how men and women in our family behave and react. You must do this. You cannot do that.

Stop.

Discard the lies.

Become who you are. Who you can be. Just because nobody in your society has ever said "Boo" to a goose, it does not mean that you cannot. You can. It is far easier than you imagine.

Courage.

Become.

Be.

"Boo" is an easy word to say.

We are shaped by our thoughts; we become what we think. When the mind is pure, joy follows like a shadow that never leaves.

Buddha

March 28

Doing

The meaning of life is to find your gift. The purpose of life is to give it away.

Pablo Picasso

It is every man's obligation to put back into the world at least the equivalent of what he takes out of it.

Albert Einstein

This can only be achieved by going through our life consciously taking action.

You may reach the end of your life without "rocking the boat," but is that enough?

It is a question only you can answer and then act on. Or not.

But hurry, it may happen sooner than you expect.

What you do makes a difference. And you have to decide what kind of difference you want to make.

Jane Goodall

March 29

Thinking

Don't believe everything you think.

Robert Fulghum

When we hear the above quote for the first time, we probably don't delve into its importance. That's if we "think" about it at all.

But so much of what we think we could do without, we accept and move on to the next thing without even considering its effect on us.

However, our unconscious is tuned into all our thoughts and uses them to create our reality.

So, every negative thought sticks to us like the limescale inside a kettle.

So, please start monitoring your thoughts and focusing on choosing positive ones.

By means of shrewd lies, unremittingly repeated, it is possible to make people believe that heaven is hell – and hell heaven. The greater the lie, the more readily it will be believed.

Adolf Hitler

Negative thinking definitely attracts negative results.

Norman Vincent Peale

March 30

Being

*You are a child of the universe, no less than the trees and
the stars; you have a right to be here.*

Max Ehrmann

We are children of the universe.
You are.
You are magnificent.
You have abilities so much greater than you give yourself
credit for.
Learn to accept and love yourself.
Learn to believe in yourself and your abilities.
Learn to see and embrace your positive attributes.
Nurture them, Nurture yourself.
Love yourself.

*Be thankful for what you have; you'll end up having more.
If you concentrate on what you don't have, you will never,
ever have enough.*

Oprah Winfrey

March 31

Acceptance

*Death is a certainty, an inevitable realisation, the only
thing that we know will befall us. There are no exceptions,
no surprises; all paths lead to it.*

Mesa Selimović

Death is on its way.
Yeeha!
Get used to it.
Use the knowledge to your advantage. Don't waste your
time.
 If it were to be tomorrow, what would you do today?
What would you put in order? Who would you see or call?
How would things taste, feel, or appear to you?
Surely, you would take an extra second or two to savour
your day as you went through it. And you would undoubtedly
feel the benefits of actually living through it wholly.
So...
It'd be a good day, wouldn't it?
Don't cheat yourself out of it today.

Death maybe the greatest of all human blessings.

Socrates

The
truth
will set
you
free

April 1

Self-worth

If you engage too much in outside validation, you lose the path to yourself.

Wim Hof

So easy to be trapped in the illusion of what others think about you.

After all, we are trained to believe what is important as children at school and at home. The chains that bind us to it are solid.

However, true validation, praise and recognition must come from within ourselves.

Praise yourself, hug yourself, and pat yourself on the back. Refrain from giving your failures the time of day. Review, acknowledge, and focus on your success.

Become your own cheerleader.

Live.

Enjoy.

We, as a species, have unlimited power of our mind. We can make anything happen.

Wim Hof

April 2

Gratitude

I cannot teach anybody anything. I can only make them think.

Socrates

Acknowledging the good that you already have in your life is the foundation for all abundance.

Eckhart Tolle

Smile. (Thank you. Keep smiling.)

Now, think of one thing you are grateful for.

It can be anything: a person, a place, a meal, something you do. In fact, anything.

And while you smile, draw the gratitude you feel for it into your heart.

Bathe and enjoy.

Now, choose a second thing.

Embrace it as you smile and feel the wonder.

And now, choose a third thing that lights up your life. Be encompassed by it.

If you do this every morning for the rest of your life, your life will be different. Wonderful. Magical.

Let us be grateful to the people who make us happy; they are the charming gardeners who make our souls blossom.

Marcel Proust

April 3

Moving

Life would be tragic if it weren't funny.

Stephen Hawking

I'm moving house in a couple of weeks, and the house I'm moving to is an entirely different space from the one I'm living in.

So, I spend a lot of time, especially at night, trying to work out what should go where. How to use the rooms.

And I have started to pack up. All those things that have been untouched, not looked at for several years. But... well, they have memories... I might want to read that book again...

It is such a playground for turmoil, such a feast for the ego. Such high-class problems.

It occurs to me that most of us do this most of the time. Find the next thing to worry about or brood on, back and forth.

I'm not moving house today, and I know I can only live in this moment.

So, do just one thing at a time. Stop. Focus. Have a pain-free head!

Worrying is like paying a debt you don't owe.

Mark Twain

April 4

Truth

It is far harder to kill a phantom than a reality.

Virginia Woolf

We create the phantoms. They don't really exist – except in our minds.

[I'm no good at this job. They'll find out. My children don't love me.]

Such beautifully crafted lies, so elegantly structured, during moments of quiet insanity.

We do not even realise that we are the sculptor, or rather, our ego has seized its chance to weave the lies that appear so undeniably real.

And when we realise this, we have the tools to demolish the lies, should we choose to escape from them.

Beware the phantom you believe to be your friend. Do not let its lies blind you.

When you consider things like the stars, our affairs don't seem to matter very much, do they?

Virginia Woolf

April 5

Beliefs

"Time", the Captain said, "is not what you think." He sat down next to Eddie, "Dying? Not the end of everything. We think it is. But what happens on earth is only the beginning."

Mitch Albom

A few days ago, I woke up feeling odd. I took my blood pressure, and it was way too high. "I don't want to die", I said, "I'm not ready. There is still so much I want to do." And I felt quite angry.

When I was drinking and drugging 45 years ago, I was terrified of dying, but I did not want to live.

Now, I want to live, and I am not afraid of dying.

I firmly believe that I am a soul in a body, and the body will die. My soul will move on.

So anyway, here I was a couple of days ago in A&E. I think they believe that if they bore us long enough, waiting in that desolate room, we'll either die or leave. So, after four hours of waiting and being occasionally tested, I left.

I feel better now. Good enough to write this.

There's nothing to fear; it's not my day to go.

Thank you for being here to read it.

I shall not wholly die, and a great part of me will escape the grave.

Horace

Excuses

It is not the mountain we conquer but ourselves.

Sir Edmund Hillary

If you spend too much time thinking about a thing, you'll never get it done.

Bruce Lee

It is so simple.
"Could you do this, please," we ask pretty reasonably.
"Yup, yup, yup."
Their lies float smoothly into the ether.
And what happens?
No, surely not! What! No, they didn't do it!
So, what can we do?
What we always do? Which is to do it ourselves!
Perhaps if we started the whole process with, "I am about to ask you to do something when I have, if you say you will do it, can I rely on you to do it?" You may want to add a time limit, like by nightfall...
Good luck and all that.
Persevere.
Enjoy your life.
No, seriously, "Enjoy your life". No one else can do that for you.

If you really want to do something, you'll find a way. If you don't, you'll find an excuse.

Jim Rohn

April 7

Love

You'll live and get hurt.

Ray Bradbury

*Ever has it been that love knows not its own depth until the
hour of separation.*

Kahlil Gibran

I was watching an episode of Alone. A handful of people living alone near the Arctic Circle have to find food themselves to survive.

One of them trapped a young squirrel. As he approached the trap, the mother squirrel was there, poking at her dead child, jumping up and down, overwhelmed with grief.

I remember seeing a mother elephant staying with her dead child for days after her herd had moved on.

The intensity of their grief, their love, moved me enormously.

It is so amazing to see animals other than humans overwhelmed with emotion.

Love is such a fantastic thing. It is so wonderful to have and to experience it. To bathe in both the pain and the pleasure it brings.

*Truth is everyone is going to hurt you: you just gotta find
the ones worth suffering for.*

Bob Marley

April 8

Trying

What is your heart telling you to do? I don't know. Maybe you're trying too hard to hear it.

Nicholas Sparks

It's true, you are trying too hard.
Almost certainly.
In some areas of your life. You are on a do, do, do and think, think, think mission.
Stop
No, seriously, STOP.
Take a deep breath and let go of everything.
Just for a moment.
Yes! You can.
Now, with another deep, deep breath, enter the peace that resides inside you and bathe gently in it.
In your mind, quietly travel forward a month or a year and see yourself at peace.
Simply being the magnificent person you can be when you are not struggling.
When you return, smile at yourself and know you can gently achieve without the noise and struggle you have been drowning in.
Choose calm.
Enjoy.

Not too hard. Not too easy. Just right.

Balayz

Heart

*In all the world, there is no heart for me like yours. In all
the world, there is no love for you like mine.*

Maya Angelou

Think of someone you love.

Now, put your hands on your heart.

Now, thinking through or with your heart, think of the person you love.

It's different.

It has a completeness.

It is possible to think with or through your heart. You do not need to put your hands on your heart to do it.

You change the source of your thoughts.

Think about your day ahead. Think about it with your head and then with your heart.

Decide which you prefer.

Start to live with your heart.

*Let yourself be silently drawn by the strange pull of what
you really love. It will not lead you astray.*

Rumi

Cycles

You never know where life is going to take you. So everything I do, I just take it one day at a time, and it always leads you to the right place.

Kyle Massey

I keep reading and coming across things that say I am always in the right place at the right time.

There have certainly been moments in my life when everything seemed totally "wrong" – a disaster, an awfulness. A, let us curl up into the smallest bug and hope that someone treads on us soon, moment. A, get me out of here, scream.

And yet...

I am still here.

I've learnt and am more human and available to help others because of my journey.

And if now, I am in the right place, at the right time, and I acknowledge and accept that, it makes whatever I am going through easier.

It changes it.

It's only those who do nothing that make no mistakes, I suppose.

Joseph Conrad

The question is not how to get cured, but how to live.

Joseph Conrad

Compliments

I can live for two months on a good compliment.

Mark Twain

When someone pays you a compliment, accept it. Say, thank you even if you do not believe it or think it is not the truth. You may not know things about yourself that others can see.

So say thank you and let the idea that what they say might be true flutter around in your head.

Say thank you and begin to own the attribute they are complimenting you on.

Say thank you and grow into the person you can be.

Say thank you and enjoy.

And compliment others about anything you can, as often as possible. Say it as if you mean it. Mean what you say. Become a champion compliment giver.

Create joy!

Nothing is more effective than sincere, accurate praise, and nothing is more lame than a cookie-cutter compliment.

Bill F Walsh

Compliment three people every day.

H Jackson Brown Jnr

April 12

Thoughts

Your thoughts are seeds, and the harvest you reap will depend on the seeds you plant.

Rhonda Byrne

Our thoughts create our reality. They cause us pain or joy if we allow them to.

They add bells and whistles to our pains, twisting the knife deeper and deeper into us. They crucify us with the past and ruin the future as they forecast disaster or doom.

When we allow our ego to be in charge, our thoughts cause us pain. Every feeling, good or bad, comes from what we are thinking.

But, as we surely know, we can use our inner being, the inner voice, to view things through. We can live a life filled with peace, calm and happiness.

The choice is ours.

Since everything is a reflection of our minds, everything can be changed by our minds.

Buddha

Simplicity

Life is really simple, but we insist on making it complicated.

Confucius

Oh, how we love to gnaw at problems, turning them over endlessly, often as we move toward sleep.

"Keep It Simple", the slogan cries. So please "keep it simple". Let go. Let go of it. Most of our gnawing is just re-chewing the same old bits repeatedly.

Take a moment to breathe and have peace.

Take a moment to look at it. Decide and then act.

Whether or not it is the right decision does not matter. Choosing a course of action and doing it will reveal the answers you need.

But once we have decided, we can let everything else go.

We can keep it simple.

Our life is frittered away by detail. Simplify, simplify.

Henry David Thoreau

Relaxing

To have faith is to trust yourself to the water. When you swim, you don't grab hold of the water, because if you do, you will sink and drown. Instead, you relax and float.

Alan Watts

Imagine standing with a heavy cloak, its weight pressing down on your shoulders as it wraps around you.

Now imagine and feel the instant release and freedom you experience as it falls to the ground. Leaving you free and light.

That is the difference between being burdened by the insanity of your ego and the simple liberation of being in touch with and guided by your inner voice, your higher self.

Relax your shoulders. As long as your body is tense, the ego rules. Relax your shoulders and see how they have tensed up without you noticing. Relax them again. Isn't that amazing?

And so, to hear your authentic voice, your loving guide, all we have to do is relax, listen, and accept.

Your mind will answer most questions if you learn to relax and wait for the answer.

William S Burroughs

April 15

Thinking

Only thoughts create. Emotions navigate.

Anthon St Maarten

My thoughts create my feelings.
All of them.
Whether I am doing anger, self-pity, sorrow, joy, or wonder, they are all created by my thoughts before I experience them.
I had probably heard that, or something like it, for years and just thought, "Oh yeah..." and dismissed it and got on with my day.
Then, one day, like a blind man who has suddenly been given sight, I took it in. I accepted it. I understood. My world shook, and it changed.
And this is the exciting news, I can choose what I want to think about.
I recommend it.
Live.
Enjoy.

Just as the ocean has waves or the sun has rays, so the mind's own radiance is its thoughts and emotions.

Sogyal Rinpoche

April 16

Awareness

There is no truth. There is only perception.

Gustave Flaubert

Think for a moment about the rest of your day, looking at it as it happens. And as you reach the end of it, notice how you feel. Then come back to now.

And now imagine that this is your first day ever, as you, in your world. Look around and notice all the colours, objects, light, and body.

Experience them all as if you have never seen, smelt, touched, tasted, or felt them. They are all new. Wonderful.

When you have appreciated all of that, travel in your mind to the end of your day again and see how it has changed.

Come back to now.

Now imagine that this is your last day on earth. When you fall asleep tonight, that is it, gone, finished.

Go through your day doing different things, meaningful and worthwhile things. Now, decide on at least <u>one</u> thing you will do differently before you fall asleep tonight.

Do it.

Enjoy.

Miracles happen every day, change your perception of what a miracle is, and you'll see them all around you.

Jon Bon Jovi

April 17

Fear

I learned that courage was not the absence of fear but the triumph over it. The brave man is not he who does not feel afraid, but he who conquers that fear.

Nelson Mandela

Those niggles of disquiet in the back of our minds and everything else, including full-blown ghastliness. All dancing away to their unique tunes.

They are all fear.

That's all, fear.

By and large, undefined thoughts fill our brain with unrest, or even agony.

If you take a long, slow, deep breath and say to yourself, "They are just fear, fear, undefined, unreal fear," then stop, be still, calm. Feel the peace that spreads over you.

Then, decide if there is any one thing, one action you want to take or do right now to change your situation.

If there is, do it as soon as possible. If there is nothing you can or want to do, then pull the peace more tightly around you and get on with your day in harmony with the world.

Every breath we take, every step we make can be filled with peace, joy, and serenity.

Thich Nhat Hanh

April 18

Action

A year from now, you may wish you had started today.

Karen Lamb

There are times when I really don't want to do things.

Sometimes, I even buy equipment or gadgets to enable me to complete a task. The object arrives. The solution and I put it on a shelf.

The "I must do that" thought floats through my mind occasionally.

Maybe after a while, I move it onto a deeper shelf.

I was talking about this to a friend, who says he does it too.

Maybe I am not such a failure after all. Perhaps I am simply human?

Whatever you want to do, do it now. There are only so many tomorrows.

Michael Landon

April 19

Illness

*The world we see in our minds become our reality. Yes, we
have to fight against darkness every once in a while, but
those who persevere get their reward.*

J D Netto

Do you reward illness?

Most parents do. When their child is ill, they shower them with gifts, sweets, kisses, and love.

And when they are not ill, they are cross and intolerant of them.

That may be too extreme for you, but most of us have done that to some extent.

Would it not be possible to reward, praise and shower them with love when they are well and treat them as usual when they are unwell?

So here we are, we've got a headache or a cold, and we take it easy, we have treats...

Instead, praise and love yourself when you are well. Look after yourself when you feel good, and stop indulging yourself when you feel off-colour. Go on, indulge in wellness.

*Reward yourself after hard work. This will encourage you
to keep going and keep growing.*

Robert Celner

April 20

Change

When in doubt, choose change.

Lily Leung

So, you want to make some changes in your life. [That is your life, not someone else's – If they are going to make changes in their life, they must do it. It's not up to you.]

Most of us would like to change things, whether to be more organised, lose weight, restart a hobby, or stop bullying our spouse.

I do not know, you choose. Or you are already perfect, in which case, bravo!

Let's take weight loss. (That's something we can really sink our teeth into.)

Merely thinking, "I'd like to lose weight." That's not going to do it.

For change to occur, you need the gift of desperation. You want to discover deep down what and why you want to change.

You want to know how you will look and feel when you achieve it, and you want to be able to see it.

And most importantly of all, you want to fill your change, your goal, and your new behaviour with emotion. And you want to engulf yourself with that emotion every day. To keep you going, day by day.

Enjoy.

Change is painful. But nothing is as painful as staying stuck somewhere you don't belong.

Mandy Hale

April 21

Joy

It's kind of fun to do the impossible.

Walt Disney

I realised the other day that my goal in life is to make everyone I meet feel better from the experience.

Even the people that I pass on the street.

I do not believe I ever made that my aim. It just gradually became who I am.

It is exciting and wonderful. It is like the best game ever.

I smile a lot. I look people in the eye and smile. I always chat with people in shops. I want to spread a little joy wherever I go.

I recommend it.

Be kind for everyone you meet is fighting a hard battle.

Ian Maclaren

April 22

Perception

*People never learn anything by being told, they have to find
out for themselves.*

Paulo Coelho

What we see in the world and how the world appears to
us depends on how we feel.

If we go out filled with anger, the world will appear
entirely differently from how we perceive it when we go out
with love and a smile.

Nothing has changed except us. And so everything has
changed.

The negative emotion does not have to be one as strong
as anger. Any negative emotion will cloud our experience.

Thank the lord that we can choose how we feel.

Always.

The mind once enlightened cannot again become dark.

Thomas Paine

April 23

Light

There is a light within each of us that can never be diminished or extinguished. It can only be obscured by forgetting who we are.

Deepak Chopra

There is always light in the depths of despair and the total blackness that can surround us.

However hard the situation you find yourself in, it is just the pendulum swinging far out in one direction. It will swing back the other way, even when that seems impossible.

It will pass.

You have an invincible summer within you.

Real generosity towards the future lies in giving all to the present.

Albert Camus

April 24

Acceptance

The first step towards change is awareness. The second step is acceptance.

Nathaniel Branden

Acceptance.
We often fight with life, trying to control or manipulate everything. Or we sulk and withdraw, still doing things but wrapping them up in a veil of resentment.
Whereas when we let go and embrace acceptance, our struggles vanish.
It is what it is. It will either continue or change. Everything in our life is written. We have agreed to it.
Even the blackest moments have an element of light when we give up fighting and accept them. Everything changes.
Enjoy your gentle, comfortable acceptance.

Life is a series of natural and spontaneous changes. Don't resist them; that only creates sorrow. Let reality be reality. Let things flow naturally forward in whatever way they like.

Lao Tzu

April 25

Unhappiness

Man is fond of counting his troubles, but he does not count his joys. If he counted them up as he ought to, he would see that every lot has enough happiness provided for it.

Fyodor Dostoevsky

Do not be unhappy in waiting. Do not walk, meander, or dash through your day, a veil shrouding your view.

We all have moments when thoughts of unhappiness and despair, call it what you will, flutter into our heads.

I know there was a time in my life when I would grasp it with both hands, turn it into concrete and bury myself in it as deeply as possible.

One does not need to go to that extreme for it to be overwhelmingly destructive.

I still have times when it zaps me, but I know now that it is false. It is my ego tricking me towards misery.

I choose not to go there. Yes, I choose. I have a choice about where I allow my mind and feelings to take me.

So now I gently say, "No". I smile at the idea of diving in and fill myself with lightness. I choose what to do and think next.

So much nicer that way.

Sometimes your joy is the source of your smile, but sometimes your smile can be the source of your joy.

Thich Nhat Hanh

April 26

Goals

Be grateful for what you already have while you pursue your goals. If you are not grateful for what you have, what makes you think you'd be happy with more?

Roy T Bennett

Humans are goal-seeking animals. We begin to die if we do not have goals or things to look forward to.

It does not have to be a ground-breaking, earth-shattering goal. It can just be having a cup of tea next week with Angela. But whatever it is, it wants to be big enough to get us out of bed today with some joy in our hearts.

If life is a struggle, it is usually because we are consumed with the grind of today, the emptiness of today, and we are not looking towards the future.

Find a goal, make a plan, do anything, take a walk by the sea, be drawn towards it, and look forward to the next.

If you want to have a happy life, tie it to a goal, not to people or things.

Albert Einstein

Perhaps when we find ourselves wanting everything, it is because we are dangerously close to wanting noting.

Sylvia Plath

April 27

Difference

Where you spend your attention is where you spend your life.

James Clear

That is so obvious, but when did we last consider it? Most people go mindlessly with the flow.

Even if we go with the flow for most of our day, we can stop now and then and choose where we focus our attention.

We can make a difference.

A difference to ourselves and the world.

The best time to plant a tree was 20 years ago. The second best time is now.

Chinese Proverb

April 28

Memories

Love is how you stay alive, even after you are gone.

Mitch Albom

You buy a bunch of flowers, still buds, full of promise. You take them home, put them in water, and place them in your favourite spot.

They flower, and they fill your world with joy-filled perfume. You delight!

When they start to be over, you place them in the recycling bin so they may return to earth.

Your memory of them, the delight that fills you when you think of them, is how wonderful they looked when they filled your room with their fantastic colours and scent.

You do not remember them as dying or dead.

And that is what we want to do with those we love. Remember, fill ourselves with the joy and happiness we shared when they were alive.

Do not indulge in sorrow and bleak black memories. Discard those. Clasp your happiness with them to your heart.

I have so much of you in my heart.

John Keats

Death is no more than passing from one room to another. But there's a difference for me, you know. Because in that other room, I shall be able to see.

Helen Keller (who went blind aged 19 months)

April 29

Answers

Stop looking for something when something has already found you. You have been living with your eyes closed. Awaken, it's there. Take it, it's yours.

Robert M Drake

When I was a young man, someone told me that if I had a problem, I should go to a library, walk around it, pick a book at random, open it anywhere, and there would be the answer to my problem.

I have done this a handful of times, and it has always worked.

Why only a handful of times? I don't know. Perhaps I am not as clever as I like to think.

Anyway, I wanted to drop this idea into your lap today. Somehow, I guessed, you needed to hear it.

Do use it if you choose to.

The solution to most of our problems lies within us. But since we are unaware, we are unable to do anything.

Santosh Joshi

April 30

Letting Go

*If it is important, do it – every day. If it is not important,
don't do it – at all.*

J R Rim

If only someone would give us a penny every time we worried about something! We'd be millionaires.

You worry about things in the future, imagining them going badly and not achieving the success you want.

If there is nothing you can do about it now, it is unimportant. If there is anything you can do now, do it.

I suggest that from now on, you say to yourself, "That's not important." Imagine it going as well as it possibly can and let go of it.

Having let go, enjoy the peace, and get on with your day.

*If you keep giving importance to unimportant things, you
can never achieve important things.*

Mindy Kaling

Enjoying?

Please
share
and
review

May 1

Thoughts

The world, as we have created it, is a process of our thinking. It cannot be changed without changing our thinking.

Albert Einstein

It is essential that we consider what our thoughts and beliefs are doing in our lives,

Everything we do and say creates our world and how we live within it.

We may have never considered this. We may have just trundled on through our lives without ever considering that we are creating all the bad and all the good things in it.

But what we think "is" what creates our world.

And we are not imprisoned by those thoughts unless we choose to do nothing to change them.

If we think positively, lovingly, and peacefully, that is the world we create.

We are addicted to our thoughts. We cannot change anything if we cannot change our thinking.

Santosh Kalwar

Stop thinking and end your problems.

Lao Tzu

May 2

Judgement

If you didn't grow up like I did, then you don't know, and if you don't know, it's probably better you don't judge.

Junot Diaz

A coward judges all he sees by what he is.

Stephen King

Nearly all of us are brought up in a judgemental environment.

Others are better or worse, clever or stupid, good or bad. To name just a few.

And nearly everyone takes their judgements into their teenage and adult life. Adding the odd sexist belief along the way.

I want to invite you to stop.

Discard judgement. Become kind and loving. The more we practice kindness and love, the more we will receive, and our lives become lighter and more joy-filled.

Don't judge me by my past. I don't live there anymore.

Zig Ziglar

May 3

Love

Love is what we were born with. Fear is what we learned here.

Marianne Williamson

When people are hostile towards us in any way, however minor, our ego leaps to its feet, sword in hand. It screams, "Attack! Attack!" And it is effortless to follow its lead and do our best to destroy our opponent.

But suppose for a moment before you leap into battle – you take a deep breath.

And then, you allowed the idea that their hostility is a cry for help – a cry for love.

Ask your inner voice who your attacker really is. What is it that they need and want?

Our ego listens to these suggestions and screams, "Rubbish! Don't be tricked! It won't work. You'll be destroyed! Attack! Attack! Defend yourself while there is still time!"

We can choose which voice we listen to. Which course to take? We know which one will benefit us and the world the best.

I believe that every single event in life happens in an opportunity to choose love over fear.

Oprah Winfrey

May 4

Sorry

If someone says that you've hurt them, you don't get to decide that you didn't.

Anne Hamble

Do you ever say I'm sorry? Do you ever apologise for what you have done?

And if you do, what do you do next?

For many people, "I'm sorry..." is a noise they make when they have been found out or caught. When they have done something "again" that they know is disrespectful towards another.

"Hang on there. You said disrespectful... I'm not sure I'd go that far... I didn't mean to disrespect... I don't think you should look at it that way... It's just something I did... Millions of people do that, and they don't apologise..."

So, there you have it.

It is not an apology at all. It's just sorry you noticed.

It doesn't even have the honesty and decency to say, "I'm not sorry... and I'm going to do it again." With the thought of, "Stop giving me those looks. Give me a break, for God's sake!"

"I am sorry." It should mean, "I am never going to do that or anything like it again. I have decided to change my ways."

If you don't mean that, then "I'm sorry" is the worst insult we can give to anyone!

Sorry doesn't prove anything unless you mean it.

Ashley Sexton

Would "sorry" have made a difference? Does it ever? It's just a word. One word against a thousand actions.

Sarah Ockler

May 5

Perfection

A life of anybody is not perfect; there is always things that happen and that is what makes it interesting.

Kevin de Bruyne

I am not tidy. I live in a comfortable disorder. I know where everything is, but I don't see the point in wasting my time tidying it up. I feel that I have better things to do.

A friend approached me for spiritual guidance, and we got along well. He started to change, and his life improved.

After a few weeks, he came to my house and looked at my disorder, and realised he couldn't take guidance from someone who was untidy. He withdrew into himself. The shutters banged down on his head.

Which is sad, I think. If it disturbs you, I'm sorry for you.

I'm not perfect, I just do what I think is right. So if I can't fulfil people's expectations, I'm sorry, but it's not my fault.

Conchita Wurst

Change

The only way to make sense out of change is to plunge into it, move with it, and join the dance.

Alan Watts

Think for a moment about who you are and where you are. Think about what is going on in your life.

Ask yourself, "Is this what I want?"

If they are honest, nearly everyone's answer is "No." While some things in their lives may be okay with them, there are many, if not most, that they do not want.

So, here is what to do.

Change your thoughts. Change the way you see yourself.

See yourself being in and enjoying the life you want. All the good things you desire.

Repeat. And repeat. And continue to see that as your reality. Talk about that being your reality. Continue.

Yes, tomorrow afternoon, Sunday week, and this time next month, you still see this as your reality.

What you see, imagine, and believe in will become your reality.

And yes, you can. Honestly, you can. It is possible. I know.

There are far, far better things ahead than any we leave behind.

C S Lewis

In any given moment we have two options; to step forward into growth, or to step back into safety.

Abraham Maslow

May 7

God

There is more that God wants to do with our lives than what we have ever known or discovered.

Benjamin Suulola

"God knows!" We cry.

"Oh, God only knows!" We throw our hands into the air, a little grey bubble of despair bursting over our heads.

Of course, although we may never have considered it, he does. It is just that we have long since switched off our listening or hearing apparatus.

If we go into the still quietness within us, there is an answer.

It may not come to us all at once.

But if we turn it over to God and continue with our lives, the answers will come when we are ready to understand them.

Only God and I knew what I meant when I wrote it, now only God knows.

Robert Frost

May 8

Focus

Just don't give up trying to do what you really want to do. Where there is love and inspiration, I don't think you can go wrong.

Ella Fitzgerald

So many of us spend so much of our lives focusing on what we do not want.

And what do we get?

What we don't want.

So, let us change our focus.

What do we want? Or rather, what do you want? What makes you feel good? Or perhaps what would make you feel good? What excites you? What lights up your life? Who fills you with joy when you are with them?

We have spent so much time focussing on and doing what we believe we should be doing.

Stop.

Focus on what you want. Be empowered.

Enjoy.

Do not waste your time.

Love yourself first, and everything falls into line. You really have to love yourself to get anything done in this world.

Lucille Ball

May 9

Forgiveness

When a deep injury is done to us, we never recover until we forgive.

Alan Paton

To forgive is to set a prisoner free and discover that the prisoner was you.

Lewis B Smedes

Does the idea of peace of mind and comfort appeal to you?

Do you want to feel whole and at ease with yourself and the world?

Do you want any of those, or do they sound like lovely ideas but...

So, what do I do to achieve peace and comfort?

Forgive.

Forgive yourself unconditionally.

Forgive others.

That is, forgive everyone unconditionally.

Which means totally.

That's it. That is all. Embrace forgiveness and then let go.

Open your arms and allow forgiveness to flow out.

None of the condemnation you have been choking yourself with is worth it. Not the condemnation of others or yourself. This has been a chain, cutting into your being and dragging you down.

Let go. Let go. Embrace freedom.

We are not the same persons this year as last, nor are those we love. It is a happy chance if we, changing, continue to love a changed person.

W Somerset Maugham

May 10

Equality

To live anywhere in the world today and be against equality because of race or colour is like living in Alaska and being against snow.

William Faulkner

And, of course, sexuality wants to be added to that quote.

The main difficulty is that we all fear what we don't understand. We feel threatened, even if only at an unconscious level.

But in fact, a prominent example of inequality is against women. The way they are treated and paid. The lazy expectations that so many men have towards them.

They believe they are the "man of the house" as they lounge around watching sports. They believe the woman is there to run the house and to be used when they are wanted.

It ain't right!

Learn to respect and to love!

It is time for them to grow up!

Nothing is impossible. The world itself says, "I'm possible!"

Audrey Hepburn

May 11

Everything

*At any moment, the decision you make can change the
course of your life forever.*

Tony Robbins

Everything is as it is meant to be.
Everything that is meant to happen today will happen.
Everything is in its proper place.
There are no mistakes.
Even that which seems imperfect is, in fact, perfect.
Everything.

*The positive thinker sees the invisible, feels the intangible,
and achieves the impossible.*

Winston Churchill

May 12

The Sea

Your heart is like the ocean, mysterious and dark.

Bob Dylan

There is peace even in the storm.

Vincent van Gogh

We, you, are like the sea.

So much of the time, we find ourselves consumed by the uproar of the waves.

Only noticing the troubles they create. Obsessed with one piece of powerful nonsense.

We think that is what we are – just the waves, wave after wave of distress. In fact, we are the sea, not simply the waves.

We have depth, peace and power. It is there any time we choose to access it.

There is peace and love waiting to enrich our lives if we choose to recognise it.

The place where the sky and the ocean meet is where all the miracles take place. You are part of this miracle.

Hiral Nagda

May 13

Rewards

*You need to spend time crawling alone through shadows, to
truly appreciate what it is to stand in the sun.*

Shaun Hick

Reward yourself.

Stop, treat and reward yourself for all the fantastic things
you do. And particularly whenever you do anything out of
the ordinary.

Often, we weren't rewarded as we grew up.

Many of us indulge ourselves with passive rewards, like
food, TV, or vegging out. But those are not rewards. They are
just things we expect to have. (We may even reward
ourselves when we don't indulge in them.)

A reward wants to be special. To be chosen and taken. It
could be as simple as going and sitting in the garden for ten
minutes. But it wants to be recognised as a reward for
something you have done.

*Apathy is a trap. There is no challenge... so there is no
reward. Remember, there is always free cheese in a mouse
trap.*

Steve Maraboli

Listening

It is impossible to over emphasise the immense need humans have to be really listened to, to be taken seriously, to be understood.

Dr Paul Tournier

It is incredibly easy not to be present when talking to others, for our mind to flit off somewhere else.

The only way that will change is if we decide and make a commitment to listen and be fully present.

Okay, we probably can't do this with everyone. But then again, why not?

Why not listen fully? Why not be present from now on?

You cannot truly listen to anyone and do anything else at the same time.

M Scott Peck

Failure

A fault is something very easy to find in others but becomes invisible when you try to find it in yourself.

Bangambiki Habyarimana

We have traits, behaviours, and characteristics that we know are not good. Aspects of ourselves that we frown upon. And when we see them in others, our ego leaps into action, condemning them utterly.

We enlarge every aspect of their failures so we feel less bad about our own. Our ego is out of control.

We can only reign it in and change it and ourselves by changing our thoughts to love. Decide to see only love in and for the world. This will, of course, lead to love coming our way. What we give, we receive.

Fill yourself with love and bask in the joy that it brings you.

A man cannot be comfortable without his own approval.

Mark Twain

Living

If you have the opportunity to play this game of life, you need to appreciate every moment. A lot of people don't appreciate the moment until it's passed.

Kanye West

Take a long, slow breath.
Travel into your day.
And answer this question.
What will make today awesome?
Find it.
Find something.
Choose something. Something simple if that's all you can find.
Looking at the light dancing on the leaves. It can be awesome. It will be awesome. It will give you something to fill yourself with gratitude for.
Do it.
Enjoy!

We're born alone, we live alone, we die alone. Only through our love and friendship can we create the illusion for a moment that we're not alone.

Orson Welles

May 17

Adventure

Adventures don't come calling like unexpected relatives;
you have to go looking for them.

Mark Jenkins

When things go wrong or don't go as we wish, or "disaster" happens in whatever form it chooses to take, our natural response is to dive into the negative, to spot and embellish all the problems.

So, here's an idea.

Make it an adventure. You remember what adventures were like as a child. And even if you can't recall specific adventures, you know what I'm talking about.

As you travel through it, look at what is happening as an adventure to the next moment and the one beyond that. Everything changes.

Nothing lives long, only the earth and mountains.

Dee Brown

May 18

Pause

*When confronted by conflict and confusion, another
practice is to take a deep breath, pause and ask: where is
the gift in this?*

Diane Dreher

It is the silence that enables us.

In the music, it is the silence between the notes, that makes the music.

It is the space between our in-breath and out-breath that makes breathing possible.

And in our heads, we have thoughts – apparently, a constant bombardment of them at times.

But there is a pause, a silence between them. It is so short, so slight that we often have no idea it is there. But it is.

If we want peace – or perhaps just a little rest from our mind's manic ramblings, if that sounds appealing – then notice the pause, the silence, enter the gap between our thoughts and go into the silence.

Prevent the following thought from arriving.

You may only be able to stop it for a second or two at first but persevere. Spend time gently enjoying the silence.

*Through the sacred art of pausing, we develop the capacity
to stop hiding, to stop running away from our experience.
We begin to trust in our natural intelligence, in our
naturally wise heart, in our capacity to open whatever
arises.*

Tara Brach

Letting Go

*Cry. Forgive. Learn. Move on. Let your tears water the
seeds of your future happiness.*

Steve Maraboli

Yesterday, I had a row, an issue, a disagreement with a close friend.

I told another friend on the phone that we'd struggled.

"Oh, what happened?"

I was about to give my detailed account when I thought, "No," if I describe what happened, I will only keep it alive. Re-living it all.

It's far better to let go and move on. Move into a happy space.

I only mention it now in the hope that when "life" happens to you, you may realise you can choose to move on rather than indulge in more pain.

*People have a hard time letting go of their suffering. Out of
fear of the unknown, they prefer suffering that is familiar.*

Thich Nhat Hanh

May 20

Love

You are in this life to love one another.

Dalai Lama

The Dalai lama was the guest speaker at a function in California.

He approached the microphone, said, "You are in this life to love one another," and walked away.

The audience was stunned.

After a short time, he returned and said, "And if you can't find it in your heart to love one another, just don't hurt one another."

And then he left the building.

I am very little inclined on any occasion to say anything unless I hope to produce some good by it.

Abraham Lincoln

Truth

All I can do is be me, whoever that is.

Bob Dylan

All that time we waste trying to be something that we are not.

We create an image and a front so people will think better of us.

God help the social media addicts who spend hours creating 45-second clips of themselves looking stunning or doing incredible things.

God help them because although they would recognise the lie they are posting if they looked, they don't. Then, they view other people's lies and feel "less than".

But leaving them aside, have you considered what you do and say to the world to present yourself as better than you are?

I am not saying that you shouldn't make an effort, but is your effort a front you use to hide behind?

It is vital that someone other than us knows who we really are.

We swallow greedily any lie that flatters us, but we sip only little by little at a truth we find bitter.

Danis Diderot

Action

Never do today what you can do tomorrow. Something may occur to make you regret your premature action.

Aaron Burr

We can't do everything.

So often, we focus on and beat ourselves up for what we haven't done, which is understandable. But let's be honest.

We can never do everything.

So, let us start by praising ourselves for everything we have done. Praising ourselves, feeling good about all the things we have accomplished.

Then, if important things still need to be done, schedule a time to do them. And do them then. Be proud of yourself.

Try not to do too many things at once. Know what you want, the number one thing today and tomorrow. Persevere and get it done.

George Allen Snr

May 23

Thoughts

The one thing we can never get enough of is love. And the one thing we never give enough of is love.

Henry Miller

Despite all the hype about multitasking, we can only think about one thing at a time.

Which is wonderful.

If we think negative thoughts, such as fear, hatred, or anger, we can change everything by thinking of something else.

"It's not that easy" you cry. Actually, it is. Start thinking about love, peace and serenity.

Of course, negative thoughts may loop back in, but we can loop straight out of them.

Thinking negative thoughts about other people hurts us, not them.

It's not about what it is, it's about what it can become.

Dr Seuss

May 24

Ego

The ego's survival rests on our listening to it and letting its perception become our perception, too.

Karen Casey

I asked a friend to hold my dog's lead while I went into a shop. When I came out, she asked, "Why doesn't she pull on the lead?" She has an untrained dog. It believes it is the leader of the pack. I have trained my dog to walk to heel, to know that I am her leader.

And so it is with the ego.

We can let it have unbridled control over us or gently and slowly train it.

Perhaps training ourselves would be more accurate. We can turn from the ego (personal self) to the still, quiet voice within (divine self), live there, and operate with it as our guide.

Yes, I still have an ego. Yes, it sometimes controls me. But now, infrequently.

It's much nicer that way.

When it comes to training a dog, five minutes Monday through Friday is better than 30 minutes on Saturday.

Martin Deeley

May 25

Pain

The cure for pain is in the pain.

Rumi

Oh, how we rebel against that, even when we know it is true. The current pain is so raw.

Let me escape.

Let me escape.

Regardless of whether the current pain is large or small, we still do our best to run away.

When we have courage and face it, it all changes. But our ego won't let us remember that. It wants to keep the fight alive. That is how it wins and controls us.

We do not need to let the ego win.

You have to keep breaking your heart until it opens.

Rumi

Fulfilment

Those who wish to sing find a song.

Swedish Proverb

The trouble is, so many of us have no desire to sing.

We push our way through our days and lives, fighting on towards the end, without so much of a squeak of a song anywhere.

"That's not me!" You cry.

Bravo! However, I suspect that if we were able to be honest, we would realise that there are large chunks of our lives when it is us.

Even if we only waste a little bit of our day like that, is it not worth addressing? Considering? Looking at?

Are there no ways to lift ourselves, our lives and our being with a song?

[And no, for pity's sake, I am not talking about singing.]

The joy in life is his who has the heart to demand it.

Theodore Roosevelt.

I think everybody should get rich and famous and do everything they ever dreamed of so they can see that it's not the answer.

Jim Carrey

May 27

Now

Be happy for this moment. This moment is your life.

Omar Khayyam

It is our choice

I know there are ALL those troubles. ALL those weights and worries.

But what can you actually do about them NOW in this second?

Nothing.

You are reading this. Therefore, you are not dealing with anything else in your life now.

So.

This is your choice.

It is my choice what I do at this moment.

I choose to feel ease and completeness.

And so armed, with this moment in my life addressed, I can move into a new present with energy and calm. I walk through my day accomplishing whatever I need to do.

But I do not have to live in any of it, until I reach it.

Realise deeply that the present moment is all you ever have. Make the Now the primary focus of your life.

Eckhart Tolle

May 28

Perception

The pessimist sees difficulty in every opportunity; The optimist sees opportunity in every difficulty.

Winston Churchill

Problems are opportunities in disguise. When our ego is in charge, it turns life into a series of problems – always finding a way to shine the light on the worst possible way of looking at what is happening in our lives.

We do not need to succumb to this outlook on life. We can reject the ego's perspective and choose to see things as opportunities.

As we progress through our lives, we can decide to look at whatever is happening as opportunities leading to something better. A better way to enjoy life as soon as I choose to see the opportunities.

Opportunity often comes disguised in the form of misfortune or temporary defeat.

Napoleon Hill

May 29

Love

Look for the inner ANGEL in yourself. Doing good and spreading JOY can be as natural here on earth as it is in heaven.

Angie Karen

We exchange thoughts with everyone, even those we pass in the street. They have thoughts about us, however fleeting.

We have thoughts about them, even if we pretend not to notice them.

Every loving thought we have enhances the world.

If our thoughts are not loving, it may be because of some judgemental baggage from our past, in which case we can gently work at discarding this part of our programming.

Or it may be because of their state of mind, which sends its message to us with their cry for help.

Then, we can learn to shower them with love,

Envelope them with love.

We are what our thoughts have made us, so take care about what you think. Words are secondary. Thoughts live; they travel far.

Swami Vivekananda

Plans

Tell me, what is it you plan to do with your one wild and precious life?

Mary Oliver

We make plans. Sometimes they happen, sometimes they don't.

Life happens to us.

We look back at things and wish they could have been different.

Things that seemed like disasters at the time turn out to have hidden and unexpected benefits.

The thing here is that all our expectations are ego-driven.

Whereas God or the universal mind quietly leads the order in our life (or apparent disorder).

It's good to make plans. But it is unwise to expect to be able to control them.

Always plan ahead. It wasn't raining when Noah built the ark.

Richard Cushing

If you want to make God laugh, tell him your plans

Woody Allen

May 31

Loneliness

Only the lonely know the way I feel tonight.

Roy Orbison

Do you ever feel lonely?
A small wave that gently creeps over you.
Or a vast crashing, bone-shaking monster that throws you to the ground, crushed and breathless.
If you ever feel lonely, whether experiencing it now or not, come on a journey with me.
Breathe deep and slow, three times.
Then go inside. Into your core, and gently, quietly find the source, the being of your loneliness.
Draw it gently to you. And embrace it with love and calm. Accept it with love. Feel calmness with it, with love.
Bring it out with you with love, peace, and calm.
Be!

The greatest thing in the world is to know how to belong to oneself.

Michel de Montaigne

let go

let go

again

June 1

Caring

It hurts to care about someone more than they care about themselves. I can tell that story from both sides.

Taylor Jenkins Reid

The push-pull of caring. The demands, the endless circles of never doing enough. The torment of not being appreciated and the suffocating blanket of being thanked too much.

So often, the parent/child melodrama plays out pathetically for years and years. No demand ever fulfilled. No thanks ever successfully expressed.

Of course, it isn't exclusively parent-child. It can be lovers or any of the mass of student/teacher relationships.

Someone does not do what we think they should have done, and "bang", the finger of blame is stabbed so violently that the relationship dies, quite unnecessarily.

The inherent problem is lack of respect and unachievable demands.

Step away. Consider with love and respect. Re-evaluate. Start again, but differently, if you are both grown up enough to do so.

Love and respect yourself. That is most important. Do not sacrifice your self-respect.

Self-respect knows no considerations.

Mahatma Gandhi

Our self-respect does not have a price tag.

Nawaz Sharif

June 2

Peace

Nothing can disturb your peace of mind unless you allow it to.

Roy T Bennett

So much time is wasted finding fault with others. Complaining about their shortcomings or even outright hostility.

They do something, and we launch into attack mode.

All quite understandable. After all, we are "right", aren't we? Anyone can see we are right.

Except for "them", of course.

We become blind to the idea of the possibility of peace.

So here we are, back again, at choice.

We have choices. There are many choices we can make every day. We can choose to change everything over and over again.

So, now, in the face of what "they have done," we can choose peace rather than damaging ourselves because of our need to be "right."

Let go.

Let them get on.

Choose peace.

Realise it is not worth fighting over silly little things. You rarely win. So stop fighting.

Choose peace.

When you do the right thing, you get the feeling of peace and serenity associated with it. Do it again and again.

Roy T Bennett

Peace begins with a smile.

Mother Teresa

June 3

Love

It's a funny thing about life, once you begin to take note of the things you are grateful for, you begin to lose sight of the things that you lack.

Germany Kent

When I was a teenager, I sat down and talked with someone I trusted. I dumped all my negative, hatred, anger, and disappointments while he listened. When I had finished, he asked me, "What do you love?"

Unfortunately, I was only a teenager, and so it took me another twenty years or so before I could begin to shift my focus thoughts and conversations from one of blackness to one of love. From all the world's shortcomings and my shortcomings, to love, to the positive.

Now, when I am confronted with complaints, I shift the conversation to positive things. I do not indulge in fear-mongering about the latest doom forecast.

Yes, there may be things we could do differently, but indulging in the fear that goes with it only makes it worse.

Find the good. Talk it up!

Accept yourself, love yourself, and keep moving forward. If you want to fly, you have to give up what weighs you down.

Roy T Bennett

June 4

Criticism

Criticism, like rain, should be gentle enough to nourish a man's growth without destroying his roots.

Frank A Clark

Do not write, text, or email your criticisms, anger, disappointment or hatred.

Do not write negatives to anyone. Ever.

If it must be said – (and often if we allow ourselves to cool, most of it probably doesn't help the situation and is better left unsaid.)

But if it must be said, say it to them. Face-to-face whenever possible.

Anything written becomes hard, tangible evidence that can be waved or shown decades after the event as proof of your evilness, keeping the fires of their hatred burning.

If you say something verbally, you can retract, alter, or change what it meant later if that is appropriate. And you can perhaps find a way to move towards forgiveness and harmony.

Oh, and don't leave recordings of your views, either. They are just as bad as written words.

Any fool can criticize and most fools do.

Benjamin Franklin

People ask for criticism, but they only want praise.

W Somerset Maugham

June 5

Kindness

*Remember, there is no such thing as a small act of kindness.
Every act creates a ripple with no logical end.*

Scott Adams

Do we do enough for others?
Do you do enough for others?
A friend of mine who no longer has a dog (she says she is too old to get another) still takes her dog poo bag out with her on her walks. And she picks up the poo left behind by others and their dogs.

Whenever I think of her, I wonder what I can be doing for others, for all of us.

My search keeps me on my toes.

No act of kindness, no matter how small, is ever wasted.

Aesop

June 6

Handing over

The intuitive mind is a sacred gift, and the rational mind is a faithful servant. We have created a society that honours the servant and has forgotten the gift.

Albert Einstein

The EGO RULES OK!
Or so it is, nearly all the time.
And if it has never occurred to you that this need not be the case, then there is little hope of avoiding it.
But changing that, changing the way we function, is not difficult. In fact, it is easy.
Before we do or think anything, all we have to do is invite our other voice, our quiet inner voice, to change what we want to do or think.
Maybe take a breath and ask, "What are the alternatives? How could I go about this differently? How can I do this in a state of peace?"
The answer, the gentle calm, will come into your mind and being.

A peaceful mind generates power.

Norman Vincent Peale

Simple life and peaceful mind are very close friends.

Mehmet Murat Ildan

June 7

Letting Go

*Stubborn and ardent clinging to one's opinion is the best
proof of stupidity.*

Michel de Montaigne

In Sydney Banks's book "In Quest of the Pearl", there is a
story about a man who loves his old shoes. When the left one
gets a hole, he buys a new pair. He leaves the shop wearing
one new shoe and one old one, carrying the others in a box
under his arm.

And I wondered how often we find a new idea that makes
sense and appeals to us, but despite that, we return to our
old ideas, refusing to let go of our beliefs.

Maybe we do this because we have never considered that
embracing new ideas only works if we discard our old ones.

*Once you stop clinging and let things be, you'll be free, even
of birth and death. You'll transform everything.*

Buddha

Expectations

Healing may not be so much about getting better, as about letting go of everything that isn't you – all of the expectations, all of the beliefs – and becoming who you are.

Rachel Naomi Remen

So, two questions for you.
What do you want?
What do you expect?
Are they the same?
Seriously, are the answers the same?
In truth, they rarely are the same. And what is interesting is that we seldom get what we want, and we nearly always get what we expect.
So I would like to suggest that you change what you expect in your mind so you start expecting what you want. Do this diligently, and your life will change.

Your expectations don't just influence your destiny, they determine it.

Frank Sonnenberg

Peace begins when expectations end.

Sri Chinmoy

June 9

Change

Change will not come if we wait for some other person or some other time. We are the ones we have been waiting for. We are the change that we seek.

Barack Obama

If we want to change, that is, if we want to change anything in our lives, the first thing we want to do is change our thinking.

Change the way we think.

Just as an athlete does stretching exercises before their event.

The easiest way to begin changing your thinking is with your eyes. Start to actually look at the world and see it differently. Most of the time, we never look at anything, we go through our day without ever stopping to take in what we see.

"What has that got to do with changing?"

It opens the curtains to your brain. It alerts you to the fact you are (dare I say it?) alive and want to make changes.

Go with it. Open yourself. Start to be aware of being alive.

Become aware of the subtle changes in your brain as you open yourself to possibility.

It felt so amazing to be alive I could never think of anything else.

Marty Rubin

June 10

Meditation

*If the ocean can calm itself, so can you. We are both salt
and water mixed with air.*

Nayyirah Waheed

We drink water to keep us alive. Even if the water is polluted, we still have to drink.

If a friend gives us a filter to pour the polluted water into so we have unbelievably clean and wonderful water, we would use it. Even if it meant waiting a few minutes for the water to appear, we would wait. We wouldn't mind.

The world we live in is polluted so our thoughts and our being become polluted.

If a friend gave us a filter for this, we would be insane not to use it... Even if it took a few minutes for the filter to work.

The filter your friend has is meditation.

And you would be insane not to spend the few minutes a day required to cleanse and change your world.

Meditation is magic, giving you far more time back than it takes to do it. When you are cleansed, you have a clarity you have forgotten existed.

*Meditation is a vital way to purify and quiet the mind, thus
rejuvenating the body.*

Deepak Chopra

June 11

Hurt

How ignorant can you be to hurt another person? You cannot hurt someone else without hurting yourself first.

Debasish Mridha

A friend told me of his anger toward his neighbour's cat, which kills the birds in his garden. He wanted to catch the cat and knock it on the head.

"But the cat is only doing what nature intended and taught. Despite your hatred of the cat, it is a beautiful animal."

Hating the cat damages you at your core level, not the cat. Wanting to hurt the cat is the same as hurting the cat. It fills you with poison that you neither need nor want. Love the cat. All negative thoughts damage you.

All of that is true about our thoughts and attitudes toward the people and events in our lives. Negativity, however justified, damages us.

Hurtful words are deep cuts in the heart. They may heal over time, but the scars never completely disappear.

Anoir Ou-chad

The thought caused me a good deal of grief. What a terrible thing it is to wound someone you really care for – and to do it so unconsciously.

Haruki Murakami

June 12

Importance

Each morning, we are born again. What we do today is what matters most.

Buddha.

What matters to you?

What truly matters?

When you peel away all the objects and people in your life, what really matters?

Who are you at your centre?

And are you being true to that? Are you respecting it? Are you doing all you can to encourage its continued growth?

Many of us get stuck on "he" or "she" is the only really important thing in my life. Everything I do is to make their life better.

However, if you are not being true to yourself, you cannot truly help them to the extent that you may want.

I suspect what matters is our ability to follow where our heart leads us and our ability to love ourselves. If we are not loving ourselves, we cannot love others.

The most important thing is to enjoy your life – to be happy – it's all that matters.

Audrey Hepburn

June 13

Growth

We are not creatures of circumstance; we are creators of circumstance.

Benjamin Disraeli

Never stop learning, growing, and looking at the world and your life with your eyes open wide.

It is so easy to get stuck in the habit of just going along with what happens without any thought or judgement. When things go wrong, accept your defeats with grace, with your head up, with your heart open, looking for your next adventure. Do not let things crush you and beat you down in the way they did when you were a child.

Have the courage to recognise the opportunities the world offers you when things do not go as planned or as you want them to.

When that happens, remember that you are available for something new and entirely different if you allow yourself to realise it.

People who never get carried away, should be.

Malcolm Forbes

June 14

Namaste

Namaste. It was a Nepalese greeting. It meant the light within me bows to the light within you.

Jennifer Donnelly

Namaste.
A gentle greeting.
For a while, I met and heard people using it without knowing its meaning.
Should I be using it?
Then, one day, I read, "Namaste: The spirit in me bows to the spirit in you."
And I thought, wow, that is a greeting I want to use.
So, I am gently pushing it out into the world.
With quiet love.

Namaste, a person says, and with just one word,
She acknowledges so much.
She acknowledges the existence of the soul,
She acknowledges the soul within her,
She acknowledges the souls within other people,
And she acknowledges the need to remember this holiest of holy truths often.

Sean Patrick Brennan

June 15

Soul

Don't question the tests of life. Just pass them with a fire in your soul.

Hiral Nagda

I put my hand on my heart and think – "I am not just a body."

I think – "I am not just a mind."

"I am a soul."

A soul in this body

There is peace and strength in knowing this. There is a gentle understanding of myself.

The slings and arrows of outrageous fortune cannot damage me.

This does not mean that I will not face challenges and struggles. I undoubtedly will.

There is a difference now. I have strength. I can sail through any storm, secure in the knowledge that I will travel through it.

In the past, when I encountered a storm, I could not imagine it ever ending.

I am no longer captive to this insane belief.

Man is so made that when anything fires his soul, impossibilities vanish.

Jean de La Fontaine

June 16

God

There's a God force inside of you that gives you a will to live.

Dick Gregory

God has entrusted me with myself.

Epictetus

I was brought up in the Church of England. In my twenties at church, the man giving the sermon said, "All Christians believe..." (I cannot recall what he said exactly.) I thought I don't believe that. Does that mean I am not a Christian?

When I entered treatment in my thirties, I was told that I had to believe in a God, a High Power.

I realised then that my concept of God was an old man with a long white beard sitting on a cloud. And I realised that this was rubbish. There was no way God could be like that.

Now, I believe in a God of my understanding, but there is still a part of me that thinks of the old man whenever I talk or think about God. I still think that's rubbish. When I communicate with God. I am often conflicted with the ideas from my childhood.

I only mention this in case anyone else struggles with this concept.

I believe in God, in God's power and all-embracing love. I pray to God. I know that God performs miracles through me. I accept all of that. When the image of the old man pops up, I communicate with the invisible force. So much greater than just him.

God is not anything human. God is a force, God is chaos, God is unknown, God is terror and enlightenment at the same time.

Ralph Fiennes

June 17

Reflections

*I had not thought before of this disfigured robber having
had a childhood.*

Charles Portis

As we go through our lives, who we see is ourselves.

All the people we meet are reflections of how we are. So,
if we are filled with anger, blame, or any negative emotion,
that is how the world will reflect itself to us.

All our experiences result from what we are projecting
into the world. We are getting ourselves back.

Think about how you feel now, and then see how your
interaction goes with the next person you meet.

So, learn to be contented, at peace and in harmony with
the world. And delight in the reception you experience.

*Find like-minded people who are on the same page as you,
and then lift each other up.*

Nahnatchka Khan

June 18

Moving

There is only one difference between slaughter and laughter and that's an S. It's all two sides of one thing and you got to make sure you're on the laughing side.

Ana Salote

A couple of months ago, a friend moved into her new house. New house gives the wrong impression. It was an old house that needed a vast amount of work done while they lived in it. New roof, staircase, front doors, windows, toilets, kitchen, etc., will give you an idea of the potential mayhem.

It turned out that her builder was a totally useless liar. She finally sacked him and has since discovered that most of his work needed re-doing.

One's immediate reaction to hearing his lunacy is to sue him. But my second and wiser reaction is don't sue him.

Over the years, I have met a handful of people who have sued others for varying amounts of money. The anger and emotional disruption they experienced were unbelievable. It was certainly not worth the money if they got it in the end.

So let it go. Thank God for your learning experience. Get on with your life. Be grateful for your blessings, don't feed your resentment bucket.

Live today.

Enjoy!

There is a difference between giving up and knowing when you've had enough.

Joanne Reed

A man's only got so many yeses inside him before he uses them all up.

Pat Conroy

June 19

Travel

Because when you stop and look around, this life is pretty amazing.

Dr Suess

It is better to travel hopefully than to arrive.

Robert Louis Stevenson

When I go on a long journey and want a break, a rest, or a snack, I turn off the road I am on and drive a few miles to find a suitable place to stop.

I have a peaceful picnic if I have food, coffee, etc.

If I haven't got anything, I stop at a quiet local bar or café and eat there.

I don't want to be surrounded by people charging mindlessly from one place to the next.

I want peace and quiet. Somewhere to gently meditate and rejuvenate myself.

It may add thirty minutes to my journey, but it is worth a fortune in return.

The journey is the reward.

Chinese Proverb

The real voyage of discovery consists not in seeking new landscapes, but having new eyes.

Marcel Prost

June 20

Love

If we want to fully experience love and belonging, we must believe that we are worthy of love and belonging.

Brené Brown

Which of these is most important for you?
To be able to love?
To be loved?
To realise that you deserve to be loved.
Probably the most important is to realise that we are worthy of being loved.
Although we may not know or have even considered it.
For most of us, loving or being loved is easy, to a greater or lesser extent.
But the idea that we deserve to be loved... is something else altogether.
It is so easy to push our "worthiness" down. To judge ourselves as failures in one way or another.

You can search the entire universe and not find a single being more worthy of love than you.

Buddha

And too often we forget we're worthy of our own love too.

Dhiman

June 21

Truth

If you want a healthy mind, you must feed your mind with truth.

Rick Warren

Our ego talks such rubbish. It uses a clever and cunning array of put-downs about us, sowing self-doubt and feelings of less than and failure.

There is a simple and powerful way to check its insanity.

Ask yourself, "Is this true?"

"Is it true? Is this who I am?"

So often, this simple question cuts through the rubbish we have been gabbling in our heads and leaves it all, a discarded pile on the floor.

Rather than being your thought, and emotions, be the awareness behind them.

Eckhart Tolle

June 22

Yes

The big question is whether you are going to be able to say a hearty yes to your adventure.

Raymond Carver

Can anything be sadder than work left unfinished? Yes, work never begun.

Christina Rossetti

YES!
Make YES your default setting.
Train yourself to think and say "yes" as your first response to everything that comes your way.

You may reconsider and decide that you will choose "no" this time, but only after you have processed the possible benefits of saying "yes".

If your first response is "no", you've already slammed the door on so many things without thought, with no decision process. Just "no", and you've continued to live in the blackness that is your life.

So say "yes!"
Choose "yes" whenever you can.
Enjoy your life.

The oldest shortest words –"yes" and "no" are those which require the most thought.

Pythagoras

I went into a French restaurant and asked the waiter, "Have you got frogs legs?" He said, "Yes." So I said, "Well, hop into the kitchen and get me a cheese sandwich".

Tommy Cooper

June 23

Pain

*Take chances, make mistakes. That's how you grow. Pain
nourishes your courage. You have to fail in order to
practice being brave.*

Mary Tyler Moore

As long as we can find value in the pain, there is no healing, mental, physical, or spiritual.

I know that sounds really off the wall, but why on earth would we choose to experience pain? That would be madness.

And yet, it is true. The ego loves suffering. It clings to it for dear life, finding some way to tweak it and keep it alive so we can continue to suffer.

Our only escape is to go into the peace and love always waiting inside us.

We want to start visualising being physically, mentally and spiritually well, healthy and full of joy and love.

*Fear and guilt are your enemies. If you let go of fear, fear
lets go of you. If you release guilt, guilt will release you.
How do you do that? By choosing to. It's that simple.*

Donald L Hicks

Personalities

Knowing your own darkness is the best method for dealing with the darknesses of other people.

Carl Jung

We have multiple personalities or separate selves, all pursuing separate agendas.

One wants us to be fit or eat less, while another wants to sit, watch TV, and eat cake. Another wants us to be angry and selfish, while another longs for peace and quiet.

And when we lose our temper, we can fall into the trap of believing that (and only that) is who we are.

Or we do things and find ourselves saying, "It is not like me to do that."

Acknowledging our different selves may allow us to detach from their demands, move through them into our hearts and inner being, and realise who we truly are.

If someone with multiple personalities threatens to kill himself, is it a hostage situation?

George Carlin

Your vision will become clear only when you can look into your own heart. Who looks outside dreams, who looks inside awakens.

Carl Jung

June 25

Blame

The search for a scapegoat is the easiest of all hunting expeditions.

Dwight D Eisenhower

Have you ever met anyone who says something like... "The reason things are bad in my life is because..." And they launch into all the ghastly things that have happened in their childhood, teens, schools, at work, with their partner, blah... blah... blah...

Blame, blame, blame.

I didn't get the winning lottery scratch card because I had to help with the washing up, and the bloke in front got the ticket that would have been mine.

Endless excuses and blame about how they haven't had the good luck they deserve.

They never think the problem is them, not all the other stuff.

Do you know anyone like that?

Want to enable them to enjoy their lot?

If they would choose to take command of their lives and live them responsibly, their lives would change.

All violence is the result of people tricking themselves into believing that their pain derives from other people and that consequently those people deserve to be punished.

Marshall B Rosenberg

June 26

Talking

One of the basic causes for all the troubles in the world today is that people talk too much and think too little. They act impulsively without thinking. I always try to think before I talk.

Margaret Chase Smith

Do you leave endless voice notes or telephone messages for anyone?

It is genuinely offensive to listen to someone ramble mindlessly about all of their troubles. Sending miles and miles of texts is just as bad.

Get yourself an app that allows you to record audio. Talk into that for as long as you like. Then, listen back to the moan you have recorded. Don't kid yourself it's "working through your feelings." This is a bit like carefully examining the results of diarrhoea, having missed the bowl.

If you listen, you will realise you know the answer you need to hear. You do not need to inflict it onto others.

Have respect towards them. Then, if you leave anyone messages, stop after one minute. Their lives do not deserve to be inflicted with your babble.

We know the answers to most of our troubles. Learn to listen to yourself.

Most people talk too much, and what they do say is often just noise or irrelevant gibberish designed to keep themselves entertained.

Stuart Wilde

Don't ever say stuff just because you think you should. That's the definition of an asshole.

Justin Halpern

June 27

Delusion

You know how they say grass is always greener on the other side? It is greener because you're not there.

Ekaterina Sedia

We've all heard, and even gone somewhere, where we believe the grass is greener, only to discover when we get there, it isn't, and the problem is that we are there.

If we are unhappy where we are, we want to start by changing ourselves where we are.

Discarding complaints, judgements, anger and fear. They are the things that are destroying our lives.

When we address them and begin replacing them with love and generosity, perhaps we will find a place with greener grass.

And it may even be where we already are. But if we do move, we can arrive with the new us.

Remember, the grass is always greener where you don't happen to be the neighbour.

Groucho Marx

June 28

Forgiveness

Forgiveness isn't approving what happened. It's choosing to rise above it.

Robin Sharma

True forgiveness is when you can say thank you for that experience.

Oprah Winfrey

I can forgive, but I can't forget – simply means I cannot forgive. I can pay lip service to forgiveness, but I cannot (I will not) do it. And when one looks at some of the things that have happened, it is easy to understand why people feel like that.

The truth is that if we do not forgive, we are hanging on to the anger, resentment and hatred we feel about it. About them.

And who is this hurting?

It is hurting us. It is poisoning us.

So when we forgive, when we truly forgive, it is we who benefit.

They may benefit, too, but that is not the point. The point is to liberate ourselves so we can get on with our lives with peace and joy.

So forgive.

Free yourself.

There is no love without forgiveness, and there is no forgiveness without love.

Bryant H McGill

June 29

Habits

Let today be the day you give up who you've been for who you can become.

Hal Elrod

Many people have habits of doing or not doing things they want to change.

The trouble is that there are too many. It is all too vast. They do a tiny bit in one area and quickly revert to their old behaviour because it is overwhelming.

Choose one simple behaviour you can succeed in altering, and this can be the beginning.

Decide always to place your shoes neatly when you come into the house. Or rinse your cup after you've had a cup of tea. Something straightforward.

Commit to doing it.

Do it.

Do it always. Don't miss out on it even once.

Whatever excuse you come up with, do it.

When it becomes intuitively part of who you are, you can add another.

Keep going.

Become who you aspire to be.

Do it slowly. Do it gently. Do it with love.

Drop by drop is the water pot filled.

Buddha

June 30

Selfishness

Almost every sinful action ever committed can be traced back to a selfish motive. It is a trait we hate in other people but justify in ourselves.

Stephen Kendrick

Are you selfish?
Our immediate gut-level response is probably "no".
However, if we take the time to explore a little deeper...?
And as we do?
Where does that take us?
And if we can find those little selfishnesses so easily... then are there not others, even better hidden that we might...
I don't know.
I'm not pointing any fingers.
It's just good to ask ourselves the question.
And then it is up to us to decide if we are, perchance, going to do anything about them.

Selfishness is not living as one wishes to live, it is asking others to live as one wishes to live.

Oscar Wilde

To be happy, we must not be too concerned with others.

Albert Camus

Don't
Complain

Don't
Explain

July 1

Ego

The Ego, however, is not who you really are. The ego is your self-image; it is your social mask; it is the role you are playing. Your social mask thrives on approval. It wants control, and it is sustained by power, because it lives in fear.

Deepak Chopra

Most people are not who they are. And that includes me and you.

Sometimes, we are our ego, barging our way through our lives, driven on by it.

Lacking in compassion, simply pin-balling on to the next moment of me, me, me.

It may disguise it very cleverly, enabling us to believe that what we are doing is for the benefit of others and ourselves. However, in the final analysis, it is only interested in staying in control.

We are not our ego.

Our real self has peace, light, love, calm, thoughtfulness, and serenity. We can choose it whenever we want to.

Put your heart, mind and soul into even your smallest acts. This is the secret of success.

Swami Sivananda

Procrastination

How soon "not now" becomes "never"?

Martin Luther

Someday is not a day of the week.

Janet Dailey

Do you ever put things off? Delay them? Allow them to become a blackness in the corner of your mind? Quietly filling you with dread and dis-ease? Building up without you noticing until the light in your life begins to fade.

When we do this, or some version of it, every time we think about it, we dive straight into the challenges and difficulties we have created in our minds. It gets worse. It gets darker.

Stop for a moment.

Come with me. See the finished task and the ease and comfort that accompany it. Feel the satisfaction or thrill that comes with its completion. Move now and start the task, focusing on the joy you feel when it's done.

Get started.

Do it.

Rejoice.

The secret of getting ahead is getting started.

Mark Twain

July 3

Silence

Listen to the silence. It has much to say.

Rumi

Breathe.
Concentrate on the in-breath.
Concentrate on the out-breath.
Concentrate on the gaps at the top and the bottom of the breaths.
There is peace there, and silence.
Bathe in the silence.
At the end of any thought, there can be silence. Notice it. Go into it. Learn to become part of the silence.
The space between noises is where peace and love reside. It is where we find God, God, and gentle knowing.
Silence, stillness and infinite being. A lake without a ripple. Infinitely deep.
Peace.
Learn to become part of the peace.

Listening to the eternal involves a silence within us.

Thomas Raymond Kelly

July 4

Learning

When you have done your part, it's time to release your work into the universe and let it do its part.

Maria Erving

When we want to grow something, we plant and water it, but actually, we allow it to grow. We have very little to do with how it accomplishes its task.

If we want to drive a car, we learn, and then we allow ourselves to drive it. We have very little to do with most of what we do. We allow ourselves to do it.

However, in many areas of our lives, we want to get things done, and we go on and on, poking and prying, explaining, ordering, and trying to control them in any way that occurs to us.

Learning to let go and allow ourselves and things to happen is marvellous. Just allow them space. Allow ourselves to fall asleep, exercise, eat less, and be in the present moment rather than struggling and often failing to achieve.

That the soft overcomes the hard, and the yielding overcomes the resistant, is a fact known to all, but practiced by few.

Lao Tzu

July 5

Letting go

Learning to ignore things is one of the greatest paths to inner peace.

Robert J Sawyer

Learning to ignore things is so important. It is so easy to be distracted and caught up in the newest wave of nonsense that creeps its way into our minds.

There are genuinely essential things that we do not want to ignore, such as a genuine cry for help.

But much of what grabs our attention can be ignored. And we benefit so much when we learn to focus on what is happening here, now, rather than answering the numerous murmurs from our phones or minds.

You can, you should, and if you're brave enough to start, you will.

Stephen King

Laughter

Laughter heals all wounds, and that's one thing that everybody shares. No matter what you're going through, it makes you forget about your problems. I think the world should keep laughing.

Kevin Hart

Laughter is so full of healing. I'm sure you've heard of people overcoming terminal illnesses with laughter. The wonderful thing about laughter is that it is so full of healing at every level. It is very easy to take what is happening to us so seriously. It is, after all, incredibly important.

But if we can laugh at anything, it lightens us, it lessens our burden, even if we are laughing at something completely different.

If we can find a way to laugh at our problem, challenge, or disaster, it radically alters it, and we can do and think things that just a few moments before were entirely out of our grasp.

A day without laughter is a day wasted.

Charlie Chaplin

July 7

Control

The reason many people in our society are miserable, sick and highly stressed is because of an unhealthy attachment to things they have no control over.

Steve Maraboli

There are moments. I'm not sure that is right. Should I say, "There are often extended periods in our lives when we wish we had control over everything? Most particularly over people?"

And oh, how we suffer because they do not, won't or can't!!!

But just imagine for a moment if you did have control. Over everything.

It would be endless. Not a moment's rest. And no one to blame when things did – inevitably – go wrong.

So rather than wanting to control, learn to let go. Learn to accept that things do or don't happen. Do your two pence/cents worth and get on with your life.

Turn it over to God or the universe. Be grateful that you are not in control.

Enjoy your corner of the world.

You always seek to control others when you are not in full ownership of yourself.

Cicely Tyson

July 8

Decisions

If you care about what people think about you, you will end up being their slave. Reject and pull your own rope.

Oscar Auliq-Ice

The decisions we make are not binding.

We can hesitate with fear before we make any decision that looms large in our minds.

All the "what ifs" flying around us like a swarm of gnats.

And since we are talking about decisions, what about the ones we made years ago that we still live with?

Let's repeat the opening statement – decisions we make are not binding. The world will not end if we change our minds. Yes, both the change and the consequences of the change can be challenging, but we will survive. There is a way through.

So courage.

Make the decisions you want to make, and go through with them. Life is an adventure. Don't die living a life of regret.

Trust your instincts, and make judgements on what your heart tells you. The heart will not betray you.

David Gemmell

July 9

Behaviour

*I learned the way a monkey learns – by watching its
parents.*

Prince Charles

So much of our being is inherited, whether we want it or
not.

Perhaps now that we are older than we were, it is time to
choose what we actually want.

Consider what behaviours, beliefs, and thought patterns
we might be better off without.

Just a thought.

You are not locked into being the way you are today.

You have a choice.

*One must think like a hero to behave like a merely decent
human being.*

May Sarton

*Man is defined as a human being and woman as a female –
whenever she behaves as a human being, she is said to
imitate the male.*

Simone de Beauvoir

July 10

Time

Ordinary riches can be stolen; real riches cannot. In your soul are infinitely precious things that cannot be taken from you.

Oscar Wilde

What is the most precious thing in your life? Your partner, children, parents, Ferrari, ring, music collection, purple sweatshirt, football team, your drink or drug? Which?

The answer, of course, is your time, it is irreplaceable.

And yet, most of us squander vast chunks of it without considering it.

We want to be mindful of how we spend it and who we spend it with. We want to feel the benefits we get from how we share it.

There is such a difference between being with someone for an hour because that is what we have to do and being present in the moment with them – being alive.

And that goes for everything we do.

Memories were certainly more precious than those worldly things. They could not be taken away by anyone.

Neelam Saxena Chandra

Doing

*As I get older, I realise just because I'm invited doesn't
mean I have to accept.*

Carlos Wallace

Do you ever say you'll do something, accept invitations,
etc, only to find some way of backing out of them as they
arrive?

"It's raining."

"My toes aren't feeling too great today."

"I completely forgot, but..."

I don't know. You probably have your personal favourites.
Stop doing it.

When you say "Yes" to something, go and do it. There is
part of you that wanted to do it, or you would not have said
"Yes". So don't let fear rule your life.

There is a part of you that will feel less good if you "make
an excuse".

Or if you don't want to do something, say "No" when it is
suggested.

The world will not end.

Action is the foundational key to all success.

Pablo Picasso

July 12

Pain

*The real difficulty is to overcome how you think about
yourself.*

Maya Angelou

If you are surrounded by trouble and strife, where
everything is a struggle – here is the good news – or is it the
bad news? I don't know. It depends on what you decide.

But here it is – the news. Whatever you are going
through, you are creating for yourself.

Yes, Yes! I know the divorce, job loss, the lack of money,
the abuse from your children, your spouse, or that colleague
at work are all real.

But actually, the only reality is the one you make. It is
how you choose to deal with it.

If you dive in and scream at the black mud – that is your
choice.

And unless you choose to change how you feel now –
even when the present troubles are long gone, you will only
replace them with new ones.

Forever.

Unless or until you decide to stop being the victim of your
own making and choose to grow up. Let the troubles play out
without allowing yourself to damage yourself emotionally.

The world is beautiful.

*I no longer have any fear of pain because I'm the one
inflicting it and can decide when it stops.*

Maude Julien

Meditation

I took a deep breath and listened to the old brag of my heart. I am. I am. I am.

Sylvia Plath

There are no signposts in the sea.

Vita Sackville-West

Take a long, slow, deep breath.
Hold it.
Slowly let it out.
It changes us. It calms our nerves and regulates our being. It gives us a new perspective on whatever we are doing. It provides us with a pause, a stillness, and peace.

There are a multitude of things we do throughout our day that we repeat over and over, such as getting in and out of our chairs, stopping at traffic lights, having a drink, etc.

I don't know what yours are, but take a moment to recognise a few.

Please choose one (or two) of them as an anchor, as your reminder to take that deep breath, hold it, and let it slowly out. I promise you that this will have a significant positive impact on your well-being and health.

Enjoy!

Men more frequently need to be reminded than informed.

Samuel Johnson

July 14

Freedom

If you don't know you're in prison, you're unlikely to escape.

Wayne Gerard Trotman

Sometimes, we are engulfed in struggle. All our energy is focused on our difficulties, often without any foreseeable solution.

We are just stuck in the problem.

Of course, there are degrees of this, and what you're experiencing now may be much greater or far less than that. But our focus is on the struggle. It pings around our brains.

May I make a suggestion?

Wherever you are in this moment in time, relax. Come into this moment. Feel the relaxation, the letting go, flow through your body.

Into your heart, your soul, your being. Relax. Have peace.

That "now" is all we have. The struggle is out there.

Allow the peace to fill you.

When you do face a challenge, it will be different.

You do not need to read this to do it. You can do it on your own whenever you want to.

Peace is something that comes from within. It is created by your willingness to accept yourself.

Jason Nelson

Gratitude

In ordinary life, we hardly realise that we receive a great deal more than we give, and that it is only with gratitude that life becomes rich.

Dietrich Bonhoeffer

Look around you and notice the things in your life. The furniture, the light, the clean air, everything and anything, and feel gratitude for it. Think about the people in your life, think about yourself, and let the gratitude you have build.

Feel the gratitude in your body. Simply saying that you feel grateful for something is useless.

You want to feel it throughout your whole body. Keep increasing it until it fills you.

Now, see yourself going through your day, sharing your gratitude with the world.

Imagine yourself going out with an attitude of "How can I help?" rather than "What is in this for me."

Share your gratitude, light and love.

Enjoy.

At times, our own light goes out and is rekindled by a spark from another person. Each of us has cause to think with deep gratitude of those who have lightened the flame within us.

Albert Schweitzer

Meditation

You do not to need to leave your room. Remain sitting at your table and listen. Do not even listen, simply wait, be quiet still and solitary. The world will freely offer itself to you to be unmasked, it has no choice, it will roll in ecstasy at your feet.

Franz Kafka

"Am I doing it right?"

"How do I know if it's working?"

Just a couple of questions that keep appearing when people ask me about meditation.

When I tell them that whatever they are doing is perfect, they do not hear or assimilate my words.

If you want to meditate – Do it. Don't worry about it.

Of course, your mind and your ego will interrupt your peace and silence. It's had years of practice, discovering how to do that.

But refuse to accept its noise.

Even if you only appear to achieve a few seconds of stillness, that is all you need.

Keep going. Keep enjoying. Keep believing. The peace, your peace is there.

Meditation is not about stopping thoughts, but recognising that we are more than our thoughts and feelings.

Arianna Huffington

Change

If you can learn how to use your mind, anything is possible.

Wim Hof

Ten minutes of breathing and cold showers can change everything for you.

If you shudder at the thought – I did. Cold shower – me – never! Think again.

If you google Wim Hof, he has courses, etc.

I cannot recommend them highly enough.

Use them to transform yourself.

I'm not afraid of dying. I'm afraid not to have lived.

Wim Hof

July 18

Seeing

If you make listening and observation your occupation, you will gain much more than you can by talk.

Robert Baden-Powell

A good hunter does not walk through the land looking for his prey. He scans everything before him, looking for what should not be there. He spots, for example, a dark patch, where perhaps there should not be a dark patch and looks closely to see if he is right. Sometimes, he is, and there is the animal he is hunting. More often, he realises it is just a dark patch, and his gaze moves on.

We can learn much from the hunters if we apply this to our interactions and conversations with others. If we can learn to look for what shouldn't be there in their demeanour or words and then question them, without confrontation, about what is going on, we may sometimes help them identify and talk about what is troubling them.

So many times when we meet people, we leave them before they even start talking.

Become a hunter who loves and helps.

You cannot truly listen to anyone and do anything else at the same time.

M Scott Peck

July 19

Trying

The hallmark of successful people is that they are always stretching themselves to learn new things.

Carol S Dweck

Trying is lying
Every time we use the word try we are lying.
It is that simple.
Try gives us permission to fail before we've even started.
Banish the word from your vocabulary.
Say, "Yes, I will do that" or "No, I won't do that." Either is fine, and they keep your dignity and honesty intact.
Think for a moment when someone asks you to come for a drink or a coffee, and you say you'll "Try and come." You know you're not going. And when you don't go, having said you'll "only" try, you think it lets you off the hook.
Don't try.
Do.
Or Don't do.

Only those who will risk going too far can possibly find out how far one can go.

T S Eliot

July 20

Put Downs

He may look like an idiot and talk like an idiot but don't let that fool you. He really is an idiot.

Groucho Marx

I have nothing but respect for you – and not much of that.

Groucho Marx

Don't have enemies.
Better still, don't do battle with anyone in any way.
Do not belittle or put down your opponents or rivals.
"Yeah, but!..."
I know all the things we have been taught about how to take advantage of others.

If we are bad-mouthing the competition at work, while we may get the work, we have sown seeds of distrust in our new customers.

Yes, we may have a spark of elation as we wittily put someone down, but the truth is that we are damaging ourselves.

Our friends may laugh with us and think we're funny, but at some level, they withhold themselves because they do not trust us.

When you dislike a neighbour, even if you never verbalise it to anyone, you are creating a negative field around you that will cause you trouble sooner or later.

Look for good. Find reasons to praise. Give love wherever you go. Do not have enemies.

Next time I see you, remind me not to talk to you.

Groucho Marx

Insults are the arguments employed by those who are in the wrong.

Jean-Jacques Rousseau

Loneliness

The most terrible poverty is loneliness and the feeling of being unloved.

Mother Teresa

Sometimes being surrounded by everyone is the loneliest, because you'll realise you have no one to turn to.

Soraya

I was thinking about the following before I wrote it. And I thought, "If I read this, I would not identify with it". And yet, despite that, there must be some truth in it. So here goes:-

Sometimes, occasionally, usually, very fleetingly, I feel like the smallest black pixel in a vast expanse of white. Alone. Ignored. Not thought of. Just tiny and lonely. Unloved. Unlovable. Unloving.

Usually, no sooner has this feeling arrived than I discard it. But sometimes, I drag it out. Dive into the isolated blackness.

So there you have it. You are not alone. Others feel the way you do.

Or do they?

The greatest thing in the world is to know how to belong to oneself.

Michel de Montaigne

Growth

*Why, sometimes, I've believed as many as six impossible
things before breakfast.*

Lewis Carroll

It is so important to stay alive.

To be on the lookout for new things and ideas to bring into our lives.

Do not die or fester in a swamp of the ordinary or mundane.

Please challenge yourself to find and do at least one new thing a week. And be sure to tell someone what you've done. This keeps the challenge alive.

Live.

Enjoy.

Be.

Challenge yourself. Try to shed an outgrown identity.

Sonia Choquette

Fatigue

We all grow tired eventually; it happens to everyone. Even the sun, at the close of the year, is no longer a morning person.

Joyce Rachelle

Rarely but occasionally, I am entirely without energy. I want to plonk and do nothing. Not think. Not move. Just blob.

The vague thought of "Pull yourself together" wafts slowly by, and I let it go. I see it. I know it's there, but I know I am not. I have gone. I am no longer available.

And so I wait. Calmly. Passively. And somewhere, somehow, I give myself permission to be like that. To be like that for however long it needs or takes.

And I can do that with quiet confidence. I know at a deeper level that the feelings will pass. I know that fighting it does not help me or it.

I know that having allowed myself time to travel through it, I will emerge with whatever energy I need to get on with whatever I decide to do.

And I know that I will want to do it. If I can only do it feeling dozy, that will be okay too. I have my permission to be me.

There are many things in life worth getting temporarily tired for, but there is nothing in life worth getting permanently tired for.

George Hammond

July 24

Moaning

As a kid, I grew to define what I didn't want my life to be like by sitting behind moaning women on the bus, hearing them bang on about their aches and pains, both real and imagined.

Julie Burchill

I have a friend who has a new job, and she is struggling. She calls me, sucks in a vast gob of air, opens her mouth, and shits on me without pause for fifteen minutes.

Not nice.

I say something occasionally, but she steamrollers on without listening. The truth is that she is not looking for help. She wants to wallow.

It is interesting that if I were to give her this reading, she would not recognise that it is about her.

Oh, she does want help. She knows that, which is why she calls, but she has fiddled with and broken her listening button.

When her pain is finally intense enough, she will become open to listening to change. However, her new job may have gone by then. Her main trouble is that she is "trying" to change everyone else, and it has not occurred to her to change herself.

She screams the lies she beholds about everything to herself and believes them. Her ego is driving her insane as it intensifies all the negative feelings. It is a shame that she cannot view the world with her heart instead.

I'm not going to hold my breath because life goes on. Life is too short to sit around moaning about what could have been or what was.

Tina Weymouth

Love is not the dying moan of a distant violin – it's the triumphant twang of a bedspring.

S J Perelman

July 25

Respect

*The self that represents me in society is a combination of
what I am, what I think I am and what I pretend to be.*

Giannis Delimitsos

Keeping track of who we are and who we present to the
world is important.

If we lie about ourselves for too long, too convincingly, we
can become so entrenched in the lie that we believe it.

For our sanity and peace of mind, it is important to
remember who we truly are and talk about that occasionally
with at least one other person.

We do not want to die so encased in our lies that we can
no longer respect ourselves.

We deserve better than that.

A monster is a person who has stopped pretending.

Colson Whitehead

*A genuine smile is the one you get from your dear old mum
as you walk down the path towards the care home on a
Sunday afternoon. A fake smile is the one you give her back.*

Rob Brydon

July 26

Distraction

When you fully focus your mind, you make others attracted to you.

Toba Beta

Here's an idea.

I know you won't do it, but the quality of your life would be so much better if you did.

When you are with someone, do not look at or use your phone.

Put it away.

Give yourself and your time to them.

Enjoy your life.

Pay attention to the things that are critical to your happiness and the happiness of others.

Israelmore Ayivor

Choice

You can't go back and change the beginning, but you can start where you are and change the ending.

C S Lewis

This may come as a surprise to you.
So buckle in.
Get ready....
Prepare yourself.
You cannot change the past.
Just in case that was too big to process, I'll repeat it.
You cannot change the past.

Yet, so many of us spend such vast energies and massive amounts of time going over the past again and again.

It must be human nature. I guess.

But the only time, the only moment that truly exists, is now. It is the one we are experiencing in this fraction of a second.

Our thoughts decide how this fraction of time will be and how we will experience it.

We must decide whether to embrace ourselves with love as we move onto the next moment, ready to make it worthwhile, or whether to persecute ourselves and draw the black shroud of negativity tightly around ourselves.

We get to choose.

And our choice affects our lives and our future.

You are responsible for your life. You can't keep blaming somebody else for your dysfunction. Life is really about moving on.

Oprah Winfrey

July 28

Love

Let me repeat one of the Holy Spirit's primary lessons:
every loving thought is true; everything else is an appeal
for healing and help, regardless of the form it takes.

Karen Casey

That statement refers to everything we think and do and everything that others think and do.

Everything.

So, if we react unsympathetically to others behaving "badly" in whatever form that takes, we increase their negativity. We are giving it something to feed on.

Whenever we choose a loving thought or action, we benefit ourselves and everyone else.

Our ego is still waiting in the wings, ready to pounce as soon as our guard is down. But we can experience peace and love whenever we choose to.

We can enjoy all the life-changing benefits that come with that.

Peace begins with a smile.

Mother Teresa

July 29

Letting Go

Some people believe holding on and hanging in there are signs of great strength. However, there are times when it takes much more strength to know when to let go and then do it.

Ann Landers

Let go.
Completely.
Now.
"What does that mean?" "How can I do that?" "Let go?"
Letting go means stopping. It means allowing others to do their own thing without interfering, offering an opinion or saying what you think.

It means being quiet, silent, and not throwing in our two pennies worth whenever we feel like it. It means not giving people unrequested advice.

Letting others live however they choose.

And the benefit for us is our unburdened journey through life.

You must learn to let go. Release the stress. You were never in control anyway.

Steve Maraboli

July 30

Peace

You cannot find peace by avoiding life.

Michael Cunningham

Think about some challenge you have coming up or about some relationship that is less easy.

Go into it and become aware of the feeling that it creates in your body. (Stop reading for a minute while you do this.)

Okay, now go into your heart. Into the peace and light in your chest. Stay there, and from there, view the challenge you are exploring.

It has changed.

It now has a calmness, a knowing that was not there.

This is the difference between thinking with your head or with your heart.

We have been locked into thinking with our heads. We can change that habit. Thinking with our hearts becomes easier every time we do it.

And we will achieve so much more because we have abandoned the battle.

The world is quiet here.

Lemony Snicket

Peace comes from within. Do not seek it without.

Buddha

July 31

Now

*Life is what happens to you while you are busy making
other plans.*

John Lennon

Now. That is all we have.

And yet, so many of us miss it nearly all the time.

I remember reading "The Power of Now" by Eckhart Tolle
and feeling my whole existence, my entire being change.

Suddenly, I had freedom and completeness for the first
time in my life.

I have re-read it many times.

I enjoy the peace and magic I experience when I am in the
"Now".

It makes such a difference. Why on earth don't I do it
more often? Perhaps I am human?

*Realise deeply that the present moment is all you have.
Make the NOW the primary focus of your life.*

Eckhart Tolle

*"What day is it?" asked Pooh.
"It's today." squeaked Piglet.
"My favourite day." said Pooh.*

A A Milne

See with

your

heart

August 1

Tiredness

Fatigue makes fools of us all.

Harvey Mackay

Sometimes, a wall of tiredness and exhaustion flows through and over me. I can feel my mind and body shutting down.

I know it isn't true. If you walked in and suggested that we do something I love, all the exhaustion would vanish faster than I could click my fingers.

However, you don't often appear with that offer.

So rather than wading on with what I'm doing, my boots full of water, the mud sucking me down, I stop.

I put three fingers together because this is what I do when I meditate. Doing it triggers the meditative state of mind. I say to myself I'm going to close my eyes for 5, 10, or 15 minutes of sleep.

When I open my eyes, I will be wide awake, full of energy, feeling as if I have had hours of deep, refreshing sleep.

I will remain wide awake and full of energy until my head touches my pillow when I go to bed.

And I do it, and it works. Always.

I also do it if I'm driving. I pull over, sleep and then continue with my journey.

Enjoy.

I meditate every day, which is profoundly restful and restorative, it wipes out any fatigue. That is my secret weapon.

Mike Love

August 2

Self-Belief

You attract whatever you give your energy, attention, and focus to. If you're thinking about it, you're magnetising it to your life – whether it's positive or negative.

Andrew Kay

We bring whatever we think about, positive or negative, into our lives. If we talk about lack and hardship, the things we don't have, then that is what we create in our lives.

The louder our moan, the stronger its fulfilment.

I have a friend who, like me, always gets a parking space wherever we go. Sometimes, often even, someone is in their car, keeping our space until we arrive.

We know there will be a parking space, so there always is.

So, beware of your thoughts.

Look for and expect what you want.

It is out there waiting for you.

Everything is energy.

Andrew Kay

August 3

Pause

*Under trees, the urban dweller might restore his troubled
soul and find the blessing of a creative pause.*

Walter Gropius

Silence is the pause in me when I am near to God.

Arvo Part

Start to harvest pauses.

If that's too big a step, start to sow some pauses into your life.

Before you do or speak: Pause.

Just for a second. Put a tiny space of nothingness between you and the next thing you do or say.

Before you pick up your phone, eat, walk out the door, sit down, get up, pay a compliment, everything or anything. Just slide a momentary pause before...

Life is different when you pause.

Life is better when you pause.

Life is more elegant.

More peaceful.

More fulfilling.

More enjoyable.

And who would not like that?

*He who can no longer pause to wonder and stand rapt in
awe, is as good as dead; his eyes are closed.*

Albert Einstein

August 4

Procrastination

You may delay, but time will not.

Benjamin Franklin

I've been driving for more than a few years, and a couple of weeks ago, I got my first speeding ticket.

It arrived, and I put it aside to be dealt with later... I know it will be easy to deal with.

It is still undealt with and is creating a black hole in my world. The black hole has started to suck other letters and routine things into it.

They say that procrastination is a posh word for sloth, but it is worse than that. It is magnificently debilitating.

It's so easy to do things straight away.

It is so much more challenging to approach the untouched mound of...

Why?

Why?

It's the job that's never started that takes the longest to finish.

J R R Tolkien

August 5

Anger

How much more grievous are the consequences of anger than the causes of it.

Marcus Aurelius

When I was in my twenties, my mother gave me her old car when she got a new one.

Some thirty years later, my mother died, and we were discussing the distribution of her belongings. My older sister screamed, "You got her car!"

So, for thirty years, she had been carrying that resentment, chalking it up, keeping it alive, throwing the odd twig on now and again to keep the fire flickering in her heart and mind.

How extraordinary.

And yet, sadly, it is not extraordinary at all. People harbour resentments, clinging to them like a rat to a plank of wood in the ocean, ensuring they never forget and enjoy every element of their anger, poisoning themselves.

All I can say is, "Please don't do that."

It is not worth it. The only person you're damaging is yourself.

Go, find someone you can talk the whole thing through with. Get rid of it. Discard it. You cannot change what happened. You can change your view about it.

Do that.

Find peace.

If you kick a stone in anger, you'll hurt your own foot.

Korean Proverb

Help

Those who are happiest are those who do the most for others.

Booker T Washington

I sit in my chair, looking at the river, watching it flow past. The sunlight from the ripples dances magically up the trees opposite. Watching the birds going carefully about their business. Cleaning, preening, and feeding themselves.

Ideas for writings fighting for a place on the page...

Sorrow, pain, fear, and joy, to mention a few.

The only way to help oneself is to help others.

The only way to bring love and light into our world is to find a way to share it. Find someone to help in whatever way is possible, and do it.

What we give, we receive, so it is up to us to go out and make the world a better place.

We can only be truly generous when we expect nothing in return.

Muhammad Ali

Help others achieve their dreams and you will achieve yours.

Les Brown

August 7

Peace

Wear the world like a loose garment, which touches us in a few places and there lightly.

Saint Francis of Assisi

We so easily, so often, bind ourselves with all the troubles in our lives as we fight ineffectually to escape.

Most troubles are imagined.

Yes, they may have a basis in reality, but our ego grabs them and dresses them up in all kinds of embarrassing costumes.

Let go.

Shed.

Take a breath and realise your foolishness. Ask your inner voice to lead you to peace.

Peace is always there.

All we have to do is change our thoughts and our focus. Realise we can walk tall alone.

Remember that when you leave this earth, you can take nothing that you have received. Only what you have given.

Saint Francis of Assisi

Judgement

Be curious, not judgemental.

Walt Whitman

We judge others constantly. Our interactions with them cause us to judge them. Even if it is only as we pass them in the street. We have inherited judgement from our families and added some more as we've gone along.

Of course, a vast amount of it is at an unconscious level, but it is there nonetheless. And somewhere inside, our babble goes on.

The solution?

To forgive ourselves for our judgement. At the same time, we want to forgive them for whatever sins we imagine they have committed.

Remember, we are always choosing what we see. We project our beliefs and ideas into the world, which is what we get back – a reflection of ourselves.

If, instead, we start to view the world and its people with love, our judgements will dissolve.

The secret of attraction is to love yourself. Attractive people judge neither themselves nor others.

Deepak Chopra

August 9

Letting Go

Ever desireless, one can see the mystery; ever desiring, one sees only the manifestations. And the mystery itself is the doorway to all understanding.

Lao Tzu

We may be searching for the truth, for the meaning of our life, but the more we struggle, the less we can understand.

Only by letting go and silently accepting can we find the open door to the truth we yearn for.

Let go and believe, and you will understand what you want to discover.

There is peace there.

Peace and ease.

You can only lose what you cling to.

Buddha

Questions

No question is so difficult to answer as that to which the answer is obvious.

George Bernard Shaw

The answer, my friend, is blowing in the wind.

Bob Dylan

So often, when asked something, people say, "I don't know."

It's just an automatic reply that requires no thought. It gets them (us) off the hook, the unconsidered response of "I don't know."

"How was Mary?" "I don't know."

"Why did you do that?" "I don't know."

"When will you be back?" "I don't know."

"How did you get on?" "I don't know."

Sometimes, it gets disguised as "I've no idea," "Mmm," or "What would you like to eat?" "I don't mind."

And the conversation ends there.

Of course, sometimes we could not care less about the answer. We ask the question to fill a space.

But often, we would like to know the answer.

So when they say, "I don't know", ask, "If you did know, what would you say?"

We can encourage them to dig deeper by asking the question again and so find an answer.

Fascinating.

The wise man doesn't give the right answers, he poses the right questions.

Claude Levi-Strauss

Gratitude

Gratitude is when memory is stored in the heart and not in the mind.

Lionel Hampton

Feeling gratitude and not expressing it is like wrapping a present and not giving it.

William Arthur Ward

I often feel overwhelmed with gratitude. I smile. It bubbles through me and out into the world. I share it wherever I go.

Is my life so much better than others? No. Better than some and certainly worse than many.

I am full of gratitude because I constantly look for things to be grateful for.

I spend time every day feeling gratitude for all my blessings. I feel gratitude in my body, feeling it is so important. It makes it real. It gives me love, healing and energy.

It's not joy that makes us grateful; it is gratitude that makes us joyful.

David Steindl-Rast

Doing

"What would you do if you were stuck in one place and every day was exactly the same, and nothing that you did mattered?"

"That just about sums it up for me."

Harrold Ramis & Danny Rubin – Groundhog Day

Oh dear.

And there is a little bit of truth in that about most of our lives.

And that is okay, I guess, provided we find some way to bring change and live in a few moments of every day.

But if not...

So many of us struggle through the "same old, same old." So much so that even our holidays are the "same old, same old."

Let's take this message as a wake-up call to do something. At least one thing that is different today.

Go On!

Live!

Curiosity is one of the great secrets of happiness.

Bryant McGill

August 13

Fear

Don't cry because it's over. Smile because it happened.

Dr Suess

*It is not death that a man should fear, but he should fear
never beginning to live.*

Marcus Aurelius

And then, there is death...
That is coming, too. That is a change. Although quite
often, it seems that we don't consider death in our plans.
Almost as if it didn't exist. Or perhaps if we don't think about
it, then it won't happen.
At one time in my life, I thought about death endlessly! I
longed for death. Anything seemed better than where I was.
And yet I was totally terrified of dying, utterly terrified.
And now?
Well, now I do not want to die. I want to live, experience,
and enjoy my life.
And I have no fear of dying.
Just a peaceful curiosity.
A gentle expectation of going home.

*For what is it to die but to stand naked in the wind and melt
into the sun? And when the earth shall claim your limbs,
then shall you truly dance.*

Kahlil Gibran

*To the well organised mind death is but the next great
adventure.*

J K Rowling

August 14

Change

We grow by making little great changes.

Michael Bassey Johnson

The butterfly effect. Kill a butterfly today, and the lack of its existence or children will ripple through the universe forever.

Everything is connected.

We are all one.

Whether we approach the situations in our day with anger or attack or walk through our day with love and understanding, the ripples will carry on in ways that we cannot begin to imagine.

You have been created in order that you might make a difference. You have within you the power to change the world.

Andy Andrews

August 15

Peace

Peace cannot be kept by force. It can only be achieved by understanding.

Albert Einstein

There can be peace.
We can contribute to it.
Peace can only start one person at a time.

How we choose to behave with others and towards ourselves alters everything.

If we go out into the world feeling, well, let's say, "hostile", then that is the environment we are creating. There will not be peace. Hostility will spread.

Of course, this starts before we even go out. If we greet our day with hostility, then it will grow.

If we start the day with gratitude and quiet reflection or meditation on all our blessings, we are likely to take this into the world with us.

We can refuse to be drawn into "hostility" when it's presented. We can sidestep it and let it float past us. We can choose peace and calm.

Those who are free of resentful thoughts surely find peace.

Buddha

August 16

Action

If you really want to do something, you'll find a way. If you don't, you'll find an excuse.

Jim Rohn

Today I will...
Go on, say it, please.
And choose something that you will do. Something different from all your yesterdays.
Something a little bit challenging.
And commit to it.
Today I will...
And tonight, as you retire having done it, pat yourself on your back. Smile with yourself inwardly and outwardly. Feel gently proud of yourself and your accomplishments.
And tomorrow, start your day with, "Today I will..."
Enjoy your life and its fullness.

It is impossible to live without failing at something, unless you live so cautiously that you might as well not have lived at all – in which case, you fail by default.

J K Rowling

August 17

Fear

Inaction breeds doubt and fear. Action breeds confidence and courage. If you want to conquer fear, do not sit home and think about it. Go out and get busy.

Dale Carnegie

Fear gets bad press. And so it should, given the devastation it causes us.

However, it can be helpful if we do not dive into it when it pokes its head up and waves to us.

We can consider why it is there, when we listen to what it says dispassionately, without letting it rip through our bodies.

There was a time in my life when everything was out of control, and whenever I got a letter that looked like a bill, I'd throw it unopened onto a table. And after a while, I could not even walk into the room with the table unless it was to throw another envelope in there.

Finally, the pain would become so great that I'd sit down with a letter opener, a wastepaper basket, and my chequebook. An hour later, I would have written a few cheques, and everything else would be in the bin.

Was I cured? Probably not. The chances were that I'd throw the next envelope onto the table when it arrived.

Although I don't do that anymore!

When we have a fear, it has a cause. If we take a few simple actions without becoming emotionally involved, the cause is dealt with, and we are free.

I enjoy being free.

He who is not every day conquering some fear has not learned the secret of life.

Ralph Waldo Emerson

Learning

None so deaf as those that will not hear. None so blind as those that will not see.

Matthew Henry

Maybe we haven't even considered the above.

Perhaps it has never occurred to us that they "are just not at home". And so we continue to pour out our wisdom – explaining why and how things should be done, or even how they "must" be done, all to no avail.

Ah well, no doubt they have been sent to us so that we can learn something.

Are we not the lucky ones to have our lessons so generously repeated?

In school, you're taught a lesson and then given a test. In life, you're given a test that teaches you a lesson.

Tom Bodett

August 19

Leaves

In every change, in every falling leaf, there is some pain, some beauty. And that's the way new leaves grow.

Amit Ray

The leaves on the trees outside my window appear in May.

It's now mid-August, and for a good few days, they have started to drop. One here and then there. Why, one wonders? Why not wait for all the others?

And then this thought... What if all the leaves in the forest dropped at the same moment?

Say, on the 21st of October, all the leaves fall.

Would you hear them hit the ground?

Makes you wonder.

Autumn leaves don't fall they fly. They take their time and wander on this their only chance to soar.

Delia Owens

August 20

Rules

*A rat in a maze is free to go anywhere, as long as it stays
inside the maze.*

Margaret Atwood

Spending the first few weeks with my delightful puppy, I realise how often I say "No" to her.

And that reminds me of the endless rules and instructions we give our children, which were once lavished upon us.

So much of who we are was inflicted on us during childhood, including our beliefs about how people behave and what is right and wrong.

The woman's place is in the home and how we treat others.

Many of those old beliefs and behaviours come from hundreds of years ago when life was vastly different.

Surely, it makes sense to look at our beliefs and behaviours and wonder if it is time to change them?

*Hypocrites are those who apply to others the standards
that they refuse to accept for themselves.*

Noam Chomsky

August 21

Forgiveness

When you forgive, you in no way change the past – but you sure do change the future.

Bernard Meltzer

A significant challenge for many people is forgiveness. Forgiving recent slights.

Though far more important and far more damaging is the inability to forgive the wrong or abuse that happened years ago in childhood.

We want to start by forgiving ourselves, even if it's just for being there when "it" happened. Our inner child/victim somehow feels responsible for what happened, even though we were only a child.

Even if, perfectly rationally, we know we are blameless.

If we want to be whole, we want to find a way to forgive them.

If we can bring ourselves to say, "... I forgive you for... I no longer want to be attached to this memory of hurt."

Forgive and find peace.

Be free.

Forgiveness is the final form of love.

Reinhold Niebuhr

August 22

Soul

There are no problems. There are only empowered solutions. Sometimes, change arrives to realign us – it always comes and goes, while dancing with our soul.

Ulonda Faye

Ashes to ashes.
Dust to dust.
Surely, that is all irrelevant.
We are a soul, a spirit, occupying this human body at the moment.
When the human body dies, the soul, our soul, travels on and continues with its adventure.
In due course, no doubt, moving into another living organism for a while.
Bodies are just the housing the spirit uses before it moves on.

Every soul is destined to be perfect, and every being, in the end, will attain the state of perfection.

Swami Vivekananda

August 23

Meditation

The most important thing is to try and inspire people so that they can be great in whatever they want to do.

Kobe Bryant

We all know that if we only eat junk food, it will make us ill. We need a balanced diet, and this is true in all areas of our lives.

If we are not meditating and having a quiet, reflective time every day, we get ill.

Just do what must be done. This may not be happiness, but it is greatness.

George Bernard Shaw

Action

Life is short. Do stuff that matters.

Siqi Chen

8760. That's a significant number. That is the number of hours you had over the last twelve months. (Add another 24 if it's a leap year).

What have you done with them?

How many have you invested wisely or celebrated unreservedly? 1%? 10%?

An hour a day?

More?

Less?

And what could you change to enhance your future?

No, the future is too big, and anyway, it never comes.

What can you do? What are you going to do today to make a difference?

Decide.

Do it.

Celebrate.

Do it again.

Success is not the key to happiness. Happiness is the key to success. If you love what you are doing, you will be successful.

Albert Schweitzer

August 25

Habits

You will enrich your life immeasurably if you approach it with a sense of wonder and discovery, and always challenge yourself to try new things.

Nate Berkus

We are so set in our ways.
We sit in the same chair.
We walk or drive the same routes.
We wear the same clothes.
We cook the same foods.
We dole out our greetings, our love, and correct behaviours.
We are stagnant.
Tear it up. Tear it all up.
Challenge yourself. Be different.
Do at least one thing today that is entirely different. Or even just slightly different. Do it with awareness. Do it fully. See, touch, feel, taste, smell, and immerse yourself in the difference.
Live.
Do something different.
And find another new thing tomorrow.
And the next day.
Until the end of time?
Live.

If there's no challenge in your life, then there's no enjoyment in your life.

David Tian

August 26

Pain

The pain is not letting it out. It is the fear of exposure.
Fear of looking, admitting, owning. Pain. So much pain.
Crippled by the secrets that we don't even know we have – so
much pain and fear.

The <u>only</u> way to move towards any light or release from
pain is to talk about it. Admit it to ourselves and someone
else.

And our reaction to that is total fear, resulting in a
massive shutdown.

So, we push it down and deny its existence.

The fear and pain married together in a hell of our own
creation.

Dare. Speak. Release.

And please, please remember to thank the pain for
leading you to do something that will finally liberate you.

Connection

I believe connection is needed more today than ever. When we allow ourselves to listen with our hearts we are then able to be truly present.

Debbie Payne

We are social animals. Interacting with others is fundamentally important to us at a core level.

So here's a couple of little challenges for you. You may do the first one regularly anyway, but today, you can do it consciously. Get someone you don't know to smile.

The second challenge is to connect with, call, or text someone you have not been in touch with for a while.

(Don't say, "I'm only doing this coz my book told me to.") Just make contact. Chat. Reconnect.

Put it on your list of things to do from time to time.

Enjoy.

The most important things in life are the connections you make with others.

Tom Ford

August 28

Accountability

Take accountability... Blame is the water in which many dreams and relationships drown.

Steve Maraboli

I did it.
Yes, I did it.
It is so important to own what we did.
To admit what we did to ourselves and others.
To take responsibility for our lives and our actions.
Moving forward is much easier because we are not trying to hide behind a veil.

Ninety-nine per cent of all failures come from people who have the habit of making excuses.

George Washington Carver

August 29

Negatives

Negative emotions are like unwelcome guests. Just because they show up on our doorsteps doesn't mean they have a right to stay.

Deepak Chopra

I have a friend who is a good actor, but his career has never really taken off. (How many actors have careers that take off? Not many, I suspect.)

However, one reason it faltered is that he decided he would never take on the role of a character who died or became seriously ill.

I think it was a wise choice. We do not want to indulge in unnecessary negative emotions, even if we only pretend to feel them. They affect our whole being.

Positive and negative emotions cannot occupy the mind at the same time. One or the other must dominate. It is your responsibility to make sure that positive emotions constitute the dominating influence of your mind.

Napoleon Hill

Freedom

Like a bird on the wire,
Like a drunk in a midnight choir,
I've tried in my way to be free.

Leonard Cohen

It's easy to spend our lives searching hopelessly for freedom, with no idea what freedom might be if we ever experienced it.

I have had lengthy periods of freedom, and I am so grateful and even honoured to have had them.

My imprisonment, which is there whenever I want it, comes when I am blindly searching for something without knowing what that might be.

Freedom is peace. I only achieve that when I stop trying to get all the pieces to fit together. When I stop trying to prove to myself, the world, and you that I am alright.

I become the headless chicken determined to get all the other chickens to behave in a way that would make them happy if only they would do it. NOW!

There's no peace there.

Peace is letting go, which is freedom.

Perfectionism is slow death.

Hugh Prather

August 31

Love

The ordinary love is a demand, the real love is a sharing. It knows nothing of demand; it knows the joy of giving.

Osho

Love is not holding on.
Love is freedom and letting go.
Love is no demands or expectations.
You have a beautiful caged bird that sings magically. You love it so, so much. If you genuinely love it, you open the cage so it may fly. Fly off and sing with freedom. If it flies away into the trees and you never see it again, do you love it any less?

Any demand, expectation, need, or dependence is not love. It is imprisonment.

Have courage.

Better to die fighting for freedom than be a prisoner all of the days of your life.

Bob Marley

Enjoy

sharing

it

with

someone

else

Doing

Stress is nothing more than a socially acceptable form of mental illness.

Richard Carlson

Do it Now!
Do it!
Jump higher!
Now!
That is how so many of us fly through our days on the call of everyone else and ourselves – a non-stop spinning from one thing to another. And even when we are not doing anything, our minds shout orders and demand our attention.

Please stop.

Very little needs to be done at once. Yes, serious accidents do need our immediate attention. But nearly everything else does not.

We have just got used to being on the do, do, do treadmill.

Please get off. Stop. Allow yourself peace. And then a bit more peace.

Decide slowly and calmly what you are going to choose to do.

The choice may even be to do nothing.

Allow yourself to live with slow elegance.

Doing nothing is better than being busy doing nothing.

Lao Tzu

September 2

Peace

Sometimes, my mind is not my friend.

Lou Sanders

Oh dear.

But how good that we are clever enough to realise that. There is hope when we can grasp that our mind is not always on our side.

We see and feel the battle within. The moment we do that, we can choose to start making a change.

We can quiet and discard the babble. We can stop and breathe and wait for the gentle knowing within us.

It is our choice.

So, it is easy.

If we choose to let ourselves explore it.

Why choose to be right instead of happy when there is no way to be right?

Hugh Prather

Change

Maybe yes comes before readiness. Maybe you say yes and then you become equipped to handle whatever is about to happen.

Glennon Doyle

Routine after routine.
We go there and back day after day. Time after time. Blinkered by familiarity.
We eat, we watch, we do.
All without having to engage because it is the same.
Deadening us.
Why?
Why?
Why?
Even if we only walked a few extra different yards and looked, immersed ourselves in the new...
We might realise that we can be alive.
It is possible.

Even the greatest was once a beginner. Don't be afraid to take that first step.

Muhammad Ali

September 4

Self-acceptance

You cannot be lonely if you like the person you are alone with.

Wayne Dyer

Like yourself.
Like yourself.
Like yourself.

Go on. It is not difficult, no matter the burden of your faults and failures.

It is possible to like yourself at your core. If you persevere, you can bring that liking up and out and encompass yourself with it.

Regardless of anything you have done or the shortcomings you perceive in yourself, you can still like yourself.

Have a gentle smile and like yourself.

Sometimes, the heart sees what is invisible to the eye.

H Jackson Brown Jnr

September 5

Advice

When you counsel someone, you should appear to be reminding him of something he had forgotten, not of the light that he was unable to see.

Baltasar Gracian

I was about to tell a friend a detailed description of a challenge I was having. He interrupted me and asked, "What would you say to someone who came to you with this?"

I started to speak, and he said, "Work it out. Think about it to the very end. Become part of the solution. Stop being part of the problem."

I did, and I realised it was not a trouble.

Nothing can dim the light that shines from within.

Maya Angelou

As we work to create light for others, we naturally light our own way.

Mary Anne Radmacher

September 6

Cycles

A tree is no more valuable than a seed. Both are simply at a different stage in their development.

J R Rim

Somehow, it is tough to imagine that your mother, your brother, your friend, whom you have just buried, will ever return. It's probably too big of an ask.

But consider, if you will, the snowflake, floating uniquely through the air, joining others, becoming snow, then water, and then vapour, patiently waiting to become a snowflake again.

Completely unique.

Maybe the process of dust to humans is not so hard after all...

We live in wonder, blaze in a cycle of passion and apprehension.

Carolyn Kizer

September 7

Trust

Sometimes you don't know who you can or cannot trust. I still learn that over and over again.

Demi Lovato

In my early twenties, I spent an hour travelling somewhere with my mother. We talked. I told her some personal things. And I assumed that they were in confidence. It did not occur to me that she would ever repeat them to anyone.

But she did! At the dinner table that night! There were lots of people there, all laughing!

I made a decision never to tell her anything again, ever.

And for twenty years, we never had a meaningful conversation.

How incredibly sad it is for both of us. We slowly learned to talk again, much later, too late.

I tell you this cautionary tale because we want to be wary of repeating what we have been told. Also, because we cannot know everything about the person we are talking to, we want to remind them that what we say is in confidence.

Trust takes years to build, seconds to break, and forever to repair.

A D Ryan

September 8

Gratitude

We need to spend some time in the weeds to appreciate the flowers.

Ed Young

More than anything in the world, we want to be appreciated. We want to be taken seriously, listened to and loved. All of which are covered by appreciated. It is our fundamental craving.

That doesn't sound too hard to achieve, does it? We could do that, to everyone we meet, couldn't we?

Appreciate them. Respect them. If only we did. If only everyone did. To everyone they met. And the ripples travelled out into the world – appreciation after appreciation.

That would make a difference.

And fill yourself with gratitude.

Everyone wants to be appreciated, so if you appreciate someone, don't keep it a secret.

Mary Kay Ash

September 9

Listening

The art of listening is not to hear what someone says but to hear how they feel.

Bob Chapman

How often do we truly listen? How often do we give ourselves wholly to the person we are with and tune into what they are feeling and saying?

The times when I do this well are when I am not thinking about what I am going to say.

Then, when they stop talking, I wait silently and open my mouth, and words come out.

The right words. Words that, if I had thought about them, I often might not have said.

The most important things to say are those which I often did not think necessary for me to say – because they were too obvious.

Andre Gide

September 10

Importance

A wonderful gift may not be wrapped as you expect.

Jonathan Lockwood Huie

What is important is not the eating, it is the tasting, the relishing.

What is important is not being with someone else but being fully with them.

What is important is not walking outside but breathing, looking, listening, and immersing ourselves in the experience.

What is important about prayer is not the requesting. It is the patient listening for the answers and the action we take after we pray.

What is important is not reading or meditating; it is the stilling of the mind and opening it to new ways of thinking and behaving. It is consciously consuming the ideas that are behind the messages.

Whoever does not know it must learn and find by experience that "a quiet conscience makes one strong!"

Anne Frank

September 11

Heart

If I create from the heart, nearly everything works; if from the head – almost nothing.

Marc Chagall

We can think with our heads or with our hearts.

Generally, without thought, we think with our heads, which is unsurprising because that is where the ego dwells.

Our ego is the insane voice, constantly shouting orders, expecting instant obedience. Our ego's goal is to be in charge. To rule our lives and everyone else's, too. It is not on our side and wants us to live a fear-filled life.

Our heart views the world with love. It is filled with gratitude and joy. It wants good things for us and all the people we meet.

It is easy to think with our hearts. To go through our day experiencing everything through our hearts and sending love and joy into the world.

How?

Just shift your mind into your heart and start to experience and live there.

This will make a dramatic and noticeable change to your experiences as you go through your day and life.

You'll never find peace of mind until you listen to your heart.

George Michael

September 12

Self-worth

Strong people have a strong sense of self-worth and self-awareness; they don't need the approval of others."

Roy T Bennett

When you leave a message on a friend's answering machine or voice note someone you know, do you start your message with... "It's only me", or "Oh, sorry to bother you!" If you do, why?

Do not start your message with an apology. It is not "only" you. It is "YOU". You are worthy of making a telephone call.

Do not start your conversations by saying sorry to bother you. You can be polite and ask, "Am I disturbing you?"

Do not insult your soul by introducing yourself as a bother! You are a worthy and magical human being. Tell them who you are and ask them to call you.

It is an absolute human certainty that no one can know his own beauty or perceive a sense of his own worth until it has been reflected back to him in the mirror of another loving, caring human being."

John Joseph Powell

September 13

Good Days

Today is a new day. Even if you were wrong yesterday, you can get it right today.

Dwight Howard

I like having good days.

So, I have a morning ritual to ensure I launch the day well.

On busy days, this may only take five or ten minutes. On days when I have the time, I may spend the best part of an hour to complete my spiritual ablutions.

I start every day by saying aloud and with feeling, "Thank you, thank you, God, help me to see things differently and to achieve whatever miracles you want of me. Help me to be energetic, enthusiastic and full of love."

I then analyse (in my mind) my daily events and visualise them having gone well.

Then, I feel gratitude for at least three things in my life, and I feel gratitude in my body.

I read one or two pages of some uplifting book and meditate for at least five minutes.

That is why my days are mostly good.

I hope everyone that is reading this is having a really good day. And if you are not, just know that in every new minute that passes, you have an opportunity to change that.

Gillian Anderson

September 14

Nothing

All there is to thinking is seeing something noticeable, which makes you see something you weren't noticing, which makes you see something that isn't even visible.

Leo Strauss

The oak tree outside my window was bare a few days ago and now has mass and solidity to its form. It is covered in green.

It is strange that the majority walking by would not notice the change. They are so wrapped up in their insular world.

King Charles II hid up an oak tree after the battle of Worcester. Enemy soldiers marched below the tree, never looking up to notice him.

The reason for this writing is that the oak tree I am looking at is actually covered with flowers. The flowers are the colour of green and pale brown leaves, but they are flowers, nonetheless.

I wonder, of those who notice that the tree is no longer bare, how many or few have the slightest notion that they are flowers and not leaves?

It makes me slightly sad.

Stop, notice, enjoy.

There's so much to appreciate about my life every single day, and I make a big point of taking time to smell the roses and noticing how lucky I am. I never want to take that for granted.

Josie Maran

September 15

Arguing

*You can't win an argument. You can't because if you lose it,
you lose it, and if you win it, you lose it.*

Dale Carnegie

Stop Arguing.
Give up creating the carefully crafted sentences you will
probably never use to put the other person down.
Stop focusing on their faults.
Give up your attack thoughts and choose peaceful ones.
Every disagreement is unnecessary. It is our ego finding
ways to pull you under by creating one negative thought after
another.
If we focus on the good things in life, on the positive
aspects of the other person, arguments will cease and leave a
space for love and caring.
When confronted, step aside. Allow the other person
freedom while you choose peace and comfort.

*When you're arguing with a fool, you're the fool for even
going back and forth.*

Justine Syke

September 16

Continuation

Love, the magician, knows this little trick whereby two people walk in different directions yet always remain side by side.

Hugh Prather

We do not die.
Our bodies cease, but we continue.
That is true of everyone. Of our parents, children, friends, and partners.
Their bodies cease, but they continue.
So be happy.
If they love you, they want you to be happy. They want you to recall them with happiness, not heart-wrenching sorrow.
Be happy.
Walk with them with joy and light in your heart.

All my life, I have made it complicated, but it is so simple. I love when I love. And when I love, I am myself.

Hugh Prather

September 17

Right Place

*Everything we touch in our daily lives, including our body,
is a miracle. By putting the kingdom of god in the right
place, it shows us it is possible to live happily right here,
right now.*

Thich Nhat Hanh

I believe that we are in the right place, at the right time, for the things happening in our lives.

And that the events are, therefore, rolling out ceaselessly.

I am sitting here today, at 11.59 a.m., writing this. I am doing it so that you, at a specific moment in time, can read this page.

And so it continues. Everything continues. Connected.

It also makes me notice the importance of my awareness as I go through my day and life.

So the bus you missed changes everything in the future.

The way I greet others, the love I feel for them and the world, or that I don't feel.

They are all so incredibly important.

*There is a destiny which makes us brothers; none goes his
way alone. All that we send into the lives of others comes
back into our own.*

Edwin Markham

September 18

Sunglasses

The world as we see it is only the world as we see it. Others may see it differently.

Albert Einstein

Years ago, my father told me about a short story he had read called "The Rose Coloured Spectacles!" It was about a man travelling down the Nile. Every day, he changed the colour of his glasses, and on the fifth day, he went mad (he probably died, I don't remember.)

I only mention this because so many people wear black or grey-lensed sunglasses, and the world looks dull through them. They do not know this, thinking it is normal. But a dark, colourless view of the world drags us down, even though we don't realise it.

So please change your sunglasses lens to brown or rose-coloured ones and see how the world improves.

Even if you're not interested in this, at least try on a pair of brown ones the next time you get the chance.

When he takes me in his arms, and speaks to me softly, I see the world through rose-coloured glasses.

Edith Piaf

September 19

Light

All the darkness in the world cannot extinguish the light of a single candle.

Francis of Assisi

Ships don't sink because of the water that is outside them. They sink because they let the water in.

And so it is with us. We sink because we allow the negatives to enter us. To consume us. To drown us.

Focus on the positive.

Refuse to allow the garbage that is so liberally scattered to affect us.

We choose what we watch. We choose what we listen to. We choose what we think.

So choose carefully.

Choose and enjoy being a light in the world.

In order to be lights, we must first be enlightened ourselves.

Sebastien Richard

Be the light and source of inspiration that others see.

Sunday Adelaja

September 20

Freedom

Why do you stay in prison, when the door is so wide open?

Rumi

Boom!

That's the question, and the answer is known only by you. It is your prison. The chains that bind you have been forged and manacled by you. Forever tightening.

That being the case, all you have to do is apply the magic words, "With one bound, he was free." To escape.

You choose how you behave today. You decide whose rules you follow. You choose the prison because there is comfort in being locked up and in blaming others. You can stop it.

No one else can free you.

You can decide to move to freedom.

I know it is scary, but the taste of freedom is genuinely marvellous. You know that. You have tasted it.

Do it again.

Now.

Freedom is choosing your responsibility. It's not having no responsibilities; it's choosing the ones you want.

Toni Morrison

September 21

Perspective

We must not allow other people's limited perceptions to define us.

Virginia Satir

It is so easy to get bogged down doing, doing, doing. Dashing from one task to another, pouring out our advice without thought, and never stopping to consider our words or actions.

Hamsters and treadmills spring to mind! And even if it is not as bad as that, we often charge through our day without a break.

So here is something to change that, if you choose to do it.

Move out of yourself (now) and look down at yourself from the ceiling on the other side of the room.

Detach.

And then, if you choose to, you can get on with what you're doing, watching yourself from up there.

It's different when we observe ourselves doing, thinking, and talking. It is impersonal. It is possible to do things without emotional involvement. Without the absolute need to be right.

One of the symptoms of an approaching nervous breakdown is the belief that one's work is terribly important.

Bertrand Russell

September 22

Self-acceptance

There is something wonderfully bold and liberating about saying yes to our entire imperfect and messy life.

Tara Brach

It is hard to accept oneself, warts and all, and feel okay about it.

Yes, we may feel good about how we see ourselves in relation to the world.

But for most of us, those moments are fleeting and clouded by the vague idea that we are not worthy.

Although we may not know precisely what it is, that we don't feel worthy of, it is just an underlying feeling of failure or lack of honest success.

These negative feelings are created in us by our ego, as it quietly whispers in the shadows that we are failures. It does not need to be specific. It knows that its power would diminish if it exposed itself fully.

So take a breath and discard your feelings of being less than and unworthy. Smile and allow the feeling of loving yourself.

You are okay.

Acknowledge it.

I learned a long time ago the wisest thing I can do is be on my own side.

Maya Angelou

September 23

Vulnerability

I always prefer to believe the best of everybody; it saves so much trouble.

Rudyard Kipling

I know there used to be a time when I viewed new people with suspicion. I did not trust them. Somewhere in the back of my mind, I had the idea that they were looking for ways to take advantage of me.

How and why has that changed?

I think it is because I now feel comfortable and at ease. Along with that feeling comes the security and the expectation that everyone will like me.

And because I assume that people will like me, I am fearless. I am invulnerable.

So I can give myself and my love to everyone I meet without worry. In fact, with confidence and openness.

I can be vulnerable and not be frightened because of my vulnerability.

Vulnerability is the birthplace of love, belonging, joy, courage, empathy and creativity. It is the source of hope, empathy, accountability and authenticity. If we want greater clarity in our purpose, or deeper and more meaningful spiritual lives, vulnerability is the path.

Brené Brown

September 24

Talking

*We sometimes encounter people, even perfect strangers,
who begin to interest us at first sight, somehow suddenly all
at once, before a word has been spoken.*

Fyodor Dostoevsky

We are part of a tribe.

Our tribe is far greater than the people we know or interact with regularly. Our tribe includes everyone we pass in the street or come into contact with, in any way.

You may have a life filled with intimate interactions, but that is not true for many. They lead insular lives.

We want to aim to improve the lives of everyone we meet. Our aim is that everyone we encounter goes away a happier, richer person because of the smile, words we exchange, or the deed we have done.

That is certainly my goal, and it is fun. It fills my life with richness.

*As you grow older, you'll find you enjoy talking to
strangers far more than to your friends.*

Joy Williams

September 25

Enough

You alone are enough. You have nothing to prove to anybody.

Maya Angelou

I am enough
You are enough.
Say to yourself, "I am enough."
Repeat it. Often. Frequently.
There is this big bucket of self-doubt that so many of us carry around all the time. Carefully, carefully, lest any splash over and get us. Again. Sh! Don't let them notice or see. Sh!
You are enough.
Say, "I am enough."
Say it with belief. Say it with light in your heart. Say it, say it, say it, until you know that it is true.
Revel in it.
You are enough.

You have a unique purpose and no one can fulfill it except for you.

Joel Osteen

Failure

Remember that failure is an event, not a person.

Zig Ziglar

How good we are at crucifying ourselves. We are masters at the art form. Take the slightest error on a good day, and we can squeeze out gallons of self-loathing for our shortcomings.

But if we stop for a moment and look honestly at it, it is something we did that was not all that bad. Certainly, nothing that deserved the death penalty.

It's just something we did. Millions have done it before us, and millions are waiting for their turn.

Let go of it.

It is not you.

You are not it.

It's okay. Life will go on. And it's better for the world to move on with a smile and a feeling of ease rather than the dreadful stupidity of self-flagellation.

Don't be afraid to make mistakes. But if you do, make new ones. Life is too short to make the wrong choice twice.

Joyce Rachelle

September 27

Choice

*There are nettles everywhere,
but smooth, green grasses are
more common still; the blue of
the heaven is larger than the cloud.*

Elizabeth Barratt Browning

Which do you focus on? Which do you notice? Which lightens up or darkens your day.

Do you live in a world that is positive or negative?

Once, my world was totally negative. It was filled with blame, anger and self-pity. A small tornado smashing its sorry way through the day.

But I've changed, thank God.

I don't really process negatives at all. I live through them for as long as I have to and then discard them.

I was reminded the other day that my beloved dog had a severe wound in her leg when she was young. I vaguely remember taking her to the vet, but that is all.

Someone asked Einstein what his telephone number was, and he had to look it up as he stated, "I don't store unimportant things in my brain".

Discard the negatives. You don't need them. They do nothing to enhance your life, only suck you into their bog. Fly with positive, with joy.

Happiness: being able to forget.

Friedrich Nietzsche

The advantage of a bad memory is that one enjoys several times the same good things for the first time.

Friedrich Nietzsche

Forgetfulness is a form of freedom.

Kahil Gibran

Words

"Well, you just don't seem very... proud of me." He started to say he was, but she interrupted him, saying, "Don't. It's like me saying you never say you love me, and you're saying it then. It doesn't matter, then. It doesn't count."

Elizabeth Berg

How do you speak to strangers or people you respect? How careful are you with what you say? How much of your criticism do you swallow before allowing it to escape?

How do you speak to your closest friends or the people you love?

Do you thoughtlessly let your put-downs escape? Is there a part of you that thinks it's okay because they know you so well?

As you consider those questions, are there things you say or do you have behaviours towards the people close to you that you want to change?

The right word at the right time will unlock the door to treasures – the wrong one will close it forever.

Rasheed Ogunlaru

Memories

You don't remember what happened. What you remember becomes what happened.

John Green

Our memories create our past, and our past creates our present. And every time we rerun the movie in our head, we make it stronger and alter it ever so slightly.

We see a past that never happened. And we create the good and bad feelings that go with the memory.

Perhaps, realising this, we can change our perspective on the past to one that is more comfortable and useful.

Certainly, persecuting ourselves does not do us any favours. Nor does it help us, in any way, to fill ourselves with hatred, anger and blame for the others involved.

As long as we are keeping the flames of revenge burning, the more deeply we are burning and hurting ourselves. Our hatred certainly does not damage them.

Let go and forgive. That is the only way to achieve personal freedom.

For to be free is not merely to cast off one's chains, but to live in a way that respects and enhances the freedoms of others.

Nelson Mandela

September 30

Being

The time for action is now. It's never too late to do something.

Antoine de Saint-Exupéry

Everything has both a beginning and an end.

When we are in "it," we easily forget that "it" will have an ending.

This applies to everything, the good and the bad things.

At the start of love with all its completeness, the idea of an ending seems impossible to imagine. Surely, this will go on and on. It is too wonderful to ever end. And yet it does. It will. Sometime.

In the middle of the dreadful things, we cannot imagine there could ever be an ending to the bog we are fighting our way through. I can assure you that the bog has an edge. You will reach it.

You will realise that "this too shall pass" is true.

Have faith, have courage. Nothing is ever as bad as we imagine it to be.

One day, you're 17, and you are planning for someday. And then quietly without ever really noticing, someday is today. And then someday is yesterday. And this is your life.

John Green

I am
responsible

October 1

Conversation

Whenever Percy stopped by to see Annabeth, she was so lost in thought that the conversation went something like this:
Percy: "Hey, how's it going?"
Annebeth "Uh, no thanks."
Percy: "Okay... have you eaten anything today?"
Annabeth: "I think Leo is one duty. Ask him."
Percy: "So my hair is on fire."
Annabeth: "Okay, in a while."

Rick Riordan

Such a vast number of conversations never happen. Yes, two or more people may be talking, but are they properly involved with what is being said?

So often, people don't tell the truth about what is going on in their lives. They are, metaphorically, hiding behind the sofa, occasionally popping their head up to contribute something and then diving back down to curse the world for its lack of caring.

Or they are standing there, talking and talking and spreading their "truth" to all who listen.

But they, themselves, are not listening. They do not care what others are saying. They may think they do, but they are driven to transmit their message. They do not have their listening and caring apparatus turned on.

So pause and consider your interactions.

Take time and love out there with you!

I think I only appear smart by staying quiet as often as possible.

Sally Rooney

Expectations

Burning bridges behind you is understandable. It's the bridges before us that we burn, not realising we may need to cross, that brings regret.

Anthony Liccione

People say, and I now believe, "You're always in the right place at the right time." Or variations of that.

Consider then the man walking to the gallows or electric chair. What about him?

And how about the carload of people in the air as their terminal crash approaches?

Are they all also in the right place at the right time? That is taking it a bit too far, surely?

Maybe it isn't if you consider the effect of their death on the people they will no longer interact with. If you think of the lessons that others may learn. Or maybe, more importantly, the interactions that others may have because "he" or "she" isn't there filling the space.

So I guess the man on death row can think, "I am in the right place. This is what is meant to be happening". And breathe a sigh of relief.

We never really get away with anything.

Ajahn Chah

So everything is something else.

Nadine Gordimer

October 3

Advice

I always advise people never to give advice.

P G Woodhouse

It is so easy to dish out advice with the certainty that it is right.

People come to us, and a light bulb moment later, there we are, airing out our unfiltered wisdom.

When I feel tempted to do this, I, sometimes on good days, think to myself, "If I were being given this advice, would I do it?"

Followed with a "Come on, be honest now!"

And then I temper my advice with that thought, if I offer it at all.

Probably the best advice is when we don't give any at all. Instead, if I can think of one, talk about what happened to someone else when they were in a similar situation.

Beware.

Just give love and support.

At the age of eleven or thereabouts, women acquire a poise and an ability to handle difficult situations, which a man, if he is lucky, manages to achieve somewhere in the later seventies.

P G Wodehouse

October 4

Fear

Don't be pushed around by the fears in your mind. Be led by the dreams in your heart.

Roy T Bennett

When I first saw that quote several years ago, I looked at it, unable to comprehend it. My fears were so consuming, and I probably had no dreams.

If I did have a dream, my fear quickly stamped it out to non-existence.

Reading it now, I find it hard to believe I can ever have been like that. And if I was – how did I change?

In those days, I had no idea it was possible to change my thoughts. I felt locked into them. But I was slowly led into a space where I could begin to understand it ever so slightly.

Learning to move from the future, where fear lives, into the present, without fear.

Just this moment. And this moment is okay.

You don't get over the fear of doing something by not doing it.

Zero Dean

October 5

Mistakes

Learn from the mistakes of others. You can't live long enough to make them all yourself.

Eleanor Roosevelt.

I know many people who do not even learn from their own mistakes. They keep repeating them and live with a look of bewildered despair spread across their faces. Or maybe a look of blind determination.

As I move toward the end of the day, I ask myself two questions. Firstly, "What went well?" This gives me a chance to praise myself. I want to feel good about how I am doing.

And secondly, I ask, "What could have gone better?" Not so that I can beat myself up, but rather to gently look at how I did.

This is where I can be mindful of repeated mistakes. These are things that I can begin to eliminate permanently from my life.

It is better to make a thousand mistakes than to think you know everything and not make any.

Paulo Coelho

October 6

Loneliness

All the lonely people
Where do they all come from?
All the lonely people
Where do they all belong?

Paul McCartney

So many lonely people. Do you know any of them? Are you one of them?

I suspect many of us suffer from an unidentified feeling of loneliness because the world has gone "digital."

Apparently, we no longer need to be with people to interact with them.

And yet virtual, electronic interaction is not real interaction. We need to be close enough to touch for it to have meaning to our core self, our being.

And our core being is what matters.

Get out there and smile, hug and touch.

There is a depth to life which only comes from our connection to other people.

Donna Goddard

October 7

Enough

Owning our story and loving ourselves through that process is the bravest thing we'll ever do.

Brené Brown

You have a unique purpose, and no one can fulfil it except you.

Joel Osteen

You are enough.
For many of us, the idea that this could be true is unbelievable.
Good enough for what?
What can I possibly hope to achieve or be?
To become the best, let's say, tennis player, the odds are 8.1 billion to one, so there is no hope there.

But let's bring that down to more manageable odds – To be the best parent, child, partner, or employee is possible.

And no one is judging you against others. You are judging yourself against the rest. What you do is unique. It may not be perfect, but it is much more than you give yourself credit for.

You are enough. You are there. You matter. You do your best. You are enough.

So be proud. Pat yourself physically on the back now!
Be magnificent.

The moment you see how important it is to love yourself, you will stop making others suffer.

Buddha

Existence

Remember me as a blur in the rearview mirror.
Was I ever there?
Did you actually see me?
I can't even see myself anymore, but here I am.

Wes Anderson

I walk through the streets, but do I exist? Are my thoughts real? How many questions can my head hold at any one time? Does any of this mean anything?

Those times in our lives when we lose ourselves. (The mid-life crisis.) Is there any truth? Or is it all just a figment of our imagination?

Of course, it isn't. We know that it is real. Don't we? But people say that we create our reality.

And if that is true, then surely the sensible thing would be to accept ourselves and the world as we perceive it.

It seems that we try to cram too much into our being simultaneously. Perhaps we could achieve peace and happiness by learning to relax and enjoy who we are.

Does the bird that is singing outside the window have any worries?

You can't wake up if you don't fall asleep.

Jarvis Cocker

October 9

Giving up

Giving up is the only sure way to fail.

Gena Showalter

Giving up. Quietly pushing it aside without even noticing that we have. Simply not doing it today. And not again tomorrow. Until we do not even notice that we are not doing it anymore.

Instead of doing it several times a week without thought, we no longer do it.

Allowing something we considered important when we started to slide quietly into non-existence.

Something that was a habit, so natural to us that not doing it was inconccivablc. And thcn, bccause of circumstances, we missed it once, then again, until we just missed them all. No longer in our life. Gone.

If we are to get them back, it will take immense effort and struggle. If we realise this and drive ourselves relentlessly, we may obtain it again.

But it requires total commitment.

Absolute commitment.

Perseverance is not a long race; it is many short races, one after the other.

Walter Elliot

October 10

Forgiveness

When a deep injury is done to us, we never heal until we forgive.

Nelson Mandela

Forgiveness is vital. Anything we are not forgiving is a negative drain that we continue to nurture in our souls, poisoning us.

Most importantly, we want to forgive ourselves. To realise who we were then is not who we are today. We are not doing "it" now. It is past.

Decide to be different if it ever happens again, and forgive yourself.

Forgiving brings light into the world. As long as you are refusing to forgive, in any area, you are damaging yourself and the world.

Forgive and be forgiven.

Now.

To forgive is to set a prisoner free and discover that the prisoner was you.

Lewis B Smedes

October 11

Friends

Be careful the environment you choose, for it will shape you; be careful the friends you choose for you will become like them.

W Clement Stone

You have two friends.

One is always complaining, moaning, pointing out all the troubles and expecting the worst. Always screaming with fear about everything and telling you what a disaster everything will be.

The other is full of light, love and excitement. Finding joy in everything, filled with hope and believing everything will turn out okay. If you are with them, and there are setbacks, they always find some way of viewing them positively.

Who do you spend your time with?

"Oh, the positive one, of course!"

But is that true? The negative one is your ego, always encouraging you to see the worst.

If you want to spend your life with the positive one, then decide to do that. Find positives in whatever you are going through.

What you concentrate on is what you manifest in your life.

No sane person would choose to focus on the negative, would they?

Sometimes, the best way to get other people to give up their ego is for you to give up yours first.

Jane Ripley

Don't massage EGOs deflate them.

Amit Abraham

October 12

Mothers

The quickest way for a parent to get a child's attention is to sit down and look comfortable.

Lane Olinghouse

Mama was my greatest teacher, a teacher of compassion, love and fearlessness. If love is sweet as a flower, then my mother is that sweet flower of love.

Stevie Wonder

Motherhood: All love begins and ends there.

Robert Browning.

On our birthday, instead of having a party and being given presents, I think the presents, the celebrations, and thanks should be given to our mother.

They are the ones who have sacrificed and suffered because of us.

They are the ones that deserve all the praise and love it is possible to give anyone.

And even if (for whatever reason) you feel like your mother doesn't deserve this, I believe you are wrong.

It's a funny thing about mothers... Even when their own child is the most disgusting little blister you could imagine, they still think that he or she is wonderful.

Roald Dahl

We are born of love; love is our Mother.

Rumi

October 13

Acceptance

Acceptance looks like a passive state, but in reality it brings something entirely new into this world. That peace, a subtle energy vibration, is consciousness.

Eckhart Tolle

Some think "acceptance" is "putting up with."

He/she does something, and we think we must accept it, whether we like it or not.

And if that is what acceptance means to you, may I suggest you do it with a smile.

Smiling as you accept something alters it. It changes its whole perspective and ours. So much better.

Acceptance doesn't mean resignation; it means understanding that something is what it is, and that there's got to be a way through it.

Michael J Fox

Acceptance and tolerance and forgiveness, those are life-altering lessons.

Jessica Lange

October 14

Self-Love

The most important thing is to enjoy your life – to be happy
– it's all that matters.

Audrey Hepburn

There was a time when I hated the world and all the people in it. But above all, I hated myself. I didn't think it would ever change.

Although you may never have been as low as that, I have talked to a vast number of people who find loving the world or themselves very hard, if not impossible. They constantly pull one stinking thing after another out of their basket, believing that is all there is.

The route to freedom comes through learning self-acceptance and self-love. Until we can love ourselves, we cannot love others.

You are okay. The lies you tell yourself are not true. You are a magnificent human being. Other people do love you. They depend on you.

You are worthy. Just think of a handful of good things and thoughts you've had today. Discard, stop focusing on your failures. Embrace the good stuff. If you can only think of one good thing, focus on that.

Slowly and gently, you will learn to love and respect yourself.

You are enough just as you are. Each emotion, everything in your life, everything you do or do not do... Where you are and who you are right now is enough. It is perfect.

Haemin Sunim

Self-love, my liege, is not so vile a sin as self-neglecting.

William Shakespeare – Henry V

Adventure

If you think adventure is dangerous, try routine; it is lethal.

Paulo Coelho

To adventure is to find yourself whole.

Tom Robbins

Be an adventurer.
Go to new places.
Do new things.
Don't starve yourself of new experiences. Eat different food. Change your routines.
Be alive.
We so quickly get stuck in the same old, same old, day after day, year after year.
Discover that being uncomfortable can be thrilling and become even more comfortable if you dare.
Instead of having the same holiday or visiting the same restaurant, ask someone half your age what they would do and do it.
Enjoy.

Every man's life is a fairy tale written by God's fingers.

Hans Christian Andersen

October 16

Trust

Timing has always been a key element in my life. I have been blessed to have been in the right place at the right time.

Buzz Aldrin

We often find ourselves going through our lives, feeling that everything is happening to us. We are being punished in some way, and more troubles come our way.

It's as if, for example, that the traffic God has got it in for us, and all the lights are red. And every idiot has been put on the road in front of us just to slow us down.

Let me make a suggestion.

Change how you view things, from happening "to" you to happening "for" you. All things are, in fact, there for your benefit.

Maybe the red lights are there so that you will get there ten minutes later, and although you do not know it, that is the right time, the best possible time for you.

Let everything happen for you, not to you.

All pieces of the puzzle need to fall in the right place to be a champion team.

Shreyas Iyer

Amends

Making amends is not only saying the words but also being willing to listen to how your behaviour caused another's pain, and the really hard part... changing behaviour.

David W Earle

We cause pain and then get on with our lives. Not giving our behaviour another thought, ignoring the wreckage spreading out behind us.

What needs to happen to make us falter and look back at the damage we have caused if we are not troubled by it? What might be enough to make us stop and consider how our behaviour has impacted the lives of others?

Usually to the lives of those closest to us. The people who put up with us, regardless of their wounds, because they love us.

Love and silence walk hand in hand.

Maybe this writing is the wake-up call we need.

The other night, I ate at a real nice family restaurant. Every table had an argument going.

George Carlin

October 18

Struggles

I tried to drown my sorrows, but the bastards learned how to swim, and now I am overwhelmed by this decent and good feeling.

Frida Kahlo

Oh, the pain while it is happening. That feeling of being unable to do anything about it and feeling swamped.

Those moments when we lose control of events, and it seems that the world and the world's friends are all conspiring to do us down.

Interestingly, when immersed in something like that, the possibility of finding a way out seems completely unobtainable.

And yet, today, when we are probably not going through any such event... We can barely remember when something like that ever happened to us.

If we could store that realisation somewhere handy, then next time everything started to fall apart, we could refuse to be swept into the bottomless gloom and despair that goes with it.

Many of us feel stress and get overwhelmed not because we're taking on too much, but because we're taking on too little of what really strengthens us.

Marcus Buckingham

October 19

Inner Voice

Everyone who wills can hear the inner voice. It is within everyone.

Mahatma Gandhi

We have an inner voice. Just waiting expectantly for our call so it can help us. Always there. Always ready, willing and eager.

However...

So many distractions!

So many. The people we are with. The thoughts in our heads spin endlessly, shouting nonsense, worry, fear, alarm, anger, sorrow, weakness, and uselessness. On and on.

So many distractions.

And we cannot have more than one thought at a time. So, the more our ego can fill us with babble, or we focus on what we think other people are thinking, the less room there is for our inner voice.

Our voice, our inner voice, is the voice of calm, peace and love. It is the voice of universal light or God consciousness. It is just waiting for us to allow it to bring smooth calmness into our minds and lives.

So turn to it and listen. Allow it to guide you to the truth, the peace, and being whole.

Your mind knows only some things. Your inner voice, your instinct, knows everything. If you listen to what you know instinctively, it will always lead you down the right path.

Henry Winkler

Night

When you're in the desert, you look into infinity... It makes you feel terribly small, and also, in a strange way, quite big.

David Lean

Our surroundings affect us.

It is so easy to live indoors. To hardly ever experience the world outside.

When did you last go out and look at the sky at night?

When, if ever, did you go to a place that is dark enough for you to be able to see the wonders of the Milky Way?

Light pollution is so vast now that 80% to 90% of us have never seen what is there.

If you want magic, go to a dark place and be dazzled by the sky.

I throw wishes into the night and wait for the stars to catch them.

Christy Ann Martine

Smiling

Always keep your smile. That's how I explain my long life.

Jeanette Calment

Jeanne Calment, born on 21st February 1875, died on 4th August 1997. Aged 122 years and 164 days.

Smiling all the way.

If you clock how you feel and then smile, you can feel a lightness spreading through you.

Play catch (or create) the smile as you walk down the street. Look the oncoming person in the eye or the face, and smile. Be radiant. Feel the smile.

See how many smiles you can collect in a day.

Have fun.

Smash it.

Enjoy.

If you have only one smile in you, give it to the people you love. Don't be surly at home, then go out into the street and start grinning "Good morning" at total strangers.

Maya Angelou

October 22

Fear

Fear can only be mastered outside of your comfort zone.

Matshona Dhliwayo

We punish ourselves with fear. Over and over again.

Fear creeps into our minds, and we run with it, adding bells and whistles as we go. Not satisfied with our fear and worry about X, we add a couple of others, Y and Z, to torture ourselves with.

You can almost see your ego leaning back in its Directors Chair as it gleefully shouts its orders.

And now, the things we fear don't even need to happen. They have already crushed us and obliterated us.

But hang on for a minute. Yes, things have gone wrong and caused us a lot of distress, but that does not mean they will happen again.

If we think about the things we worried about yesterday or last week, how many of them went as badly as we expected? Somewhere between none and very few.

What we are fearing now is not happening now. So come into the present and enjoy it.

And if it does go badly, you can deal with it then. There is no point in suffering now and as well as when it happens.

Take a deep breath. You will be fine. Where you are meant to be, you will be in time.

Morgan Harper Nichols

October 23

Love

If our love is only a will to possess, it is not love.

Thich Nhat Hanh

Possessiveness is not love. So often, we think it is. We have unwritten, unspoken rules and expectations about the person we love.

"If you loved me, you'd do this..." or "You wouldn't do that..."

Love does not have rules. Love is freedom. Love is the ability to let go.

And if you are doing or not doing things "because you love them," that's okay, as long as you can do them with love rather than suppressed irritation.

If you are complaining about your lot, you are not sharing love but rather sharing slavery.

And shared slavery is likely to end with your parting.

For love to work, we must both be able to be free and grow together, changing and enjoying our journeys.

Love and freedom are such hideous words. So many cruelties have been done in their name.

Joseph O'Connor

Mistakes

Success does not consist in never making mistakes but in never making the same one a second time.

George Bernard Shaw

Do it!
Crash on!
Keep Going.
Dare to make mistakes.
Mistakes are the lifeblood of success.

Look back at your past. All the growth, knowledge, and success have their footprints in mistakes and failures.

So stop worrying about mistakes. Don't let fear paralyse you. Discuss your journey with someone. Dare to become a glorious, beautiful flower.

Dare to fail. Live.

If we are not living, we are already dead. We just don't realise it yet.

Stop dreaming about your bucket list and start living it.

Annette White

Awareness

Embrace the uncertainty with courage and grace,
for in this cosmic adventure, amazing things take place.

Lyra Brave

As children, we wanted it NOW!
We could not bear the wait.
And that trait still haunts many of us. We want the end result and resent all the steps we have to go through to get there.

But there is a necessary order to our journey if we would acknowledge it. Also, the steps we take often lead us to other things we might miss if we got there with one step.

So be grateful for and rejoice in the journey. Notice all the treats when we take the time to notice them.

No one saves us but ourselves. No one can and no one may.
We ourselves must walk the path.

Buddha

Doing

Position yourself to succeed by doing the other things in your life that rejuvenate you. Exhaustion affects your quality and productivity.

Jeff VanderMeer

So, is your life something you "have" to do or something you "get" to do?

So many people spend their time doing things because they have to.

This makes everything a struggle. There is no fun.

Changing your mind so you're "getting" to do things changes them. It changes them to "wanting" to do them.

For example, do you go and see a movie because you "have" to? Or do you "get" to see a movie, which is a treat? Or do you even go to the movie because you "want" to? All such different experiences.

Do you go to work because you "have" to? Or do you go to work because you are lucky enough to have work to go to? Or do you go because you want to?

How about tidying your house? Is that a "have" to, "get" to or "want" to?

Choose to enjoy your life. Much more fun.

Start where you are. Use what you have. Do what you can.

Arthur Ashe

October 27

Freedom

I would like to be remembered as a person who wants to be free... so other people would also be free.

Rosa Parks

This is difficult for me to write.

And I hope that it will be difficult for you to read.

So please, before we begin, will you open your imagination for me?

Search in there to find all the answers. And find and immerse yourself in the feelings that go with this.

So here goes: Do you live now, at this moment, in a place where there is fighting, shooting and bombing?

Is there a sniper killing people every day in the street you have to walk down and back every day?

Are they dropping bombs on the train station that is less than a mile away?

Is a day when you can get food a good day?

Do you doubt that your baby will live through today?

Do you know what total all-encompassing sick-making fear is?

Everyday?

Freedom is the oxygen of the soul.

Moshe Dayan

October 28

Risks

Be brave. Take risks. Nothing can substitute experience.

Paulo Coelho

I don't take enough risks, and I know that. But somehow, realising that brings me closer to the courage and excitement of taking them.

There are so many opportunities, and each time I take one in any area of my life, it makes it easier for me to start the next one.

Starting is all I need to do to make it happen.

If you dare nothing, then when the day is over, nothing is all you will have gained.

Neil Gaiman

October 29

Rhythms

*The same stream of life that runs through my veins night
and day runs through the world.*

Rabindranath Tagore

There is a time when trees flower and a time when they
drop their leaves. They have a rhythm, a cycle. Everything
has a rhythm.

We have rhythms. Ours are much shorter than trees, but
they are there nonetheless.

There are times when we are outgoing and find it easy to
make new friends and times when we crave solitude and
withdraw. These are just two examples of our rhythms.
There are many others.

It is a good idea to be aware of your rhythms and not to
fight them. Allow your predominant feeling or mood to lead
your behaviour, rather than trying to force yourself into
doing things you do not feel like.

*Happiness is not a matter of intensity but of balance, order,
rhythm and harmony.*

Thomas Merton

October 30

Addiction

Life is like riding a bicycle. To keep your balance, you must keep moving.

Albert Einstein

We dull our senses and our lives with addiction. And I am not just referring to drugs and alcohol.

Shopping, Facebook, Instagram, TV, gaming, eating, exercising, working. The list is endless. We stop living and hand our minds over to the addiction. We no longer need to function in the way we could.

To all intents and purposes, we are already dead.

We are incredible, magnificent human beings, yet we lead our lives as if we are driving along with our foot always on the brake pedal and gripping the steering wheel. Only focussed on the twenty yards ahead of us.

This is a wake-up call. A nudge to help you start living. To start being. To become one with the world again. Before it is too late.

The man who moves a mountain begins by carrying away small stones

Confucius

The only person you are destined to become is the person you decide to be.

Ralph Waldo Emerson

October 31

Distraction

What were we hoping to get out of this?
Some kind of momentary bliss?

Conor O'Brien – Villagers

So often, we "do" in the hope of momentary bliss.

We aren't aware of that. Or if, at some level, we are aware, we do not admit it to ourselves. And certainly not to anyone else.

There is probably nothing wrong with pursuing momentary bliss unless it prevents us from engaging in the reality of what we could be doing instead.

If we look back over our day and take stock of what has happened and what we have or have not achieved, we may have a better idea about how we are spending or wasting our lives.

And then?

Well then...

Maybe we make changes?

I waited for something, and something died.
So I waited for nothing, and nothing arrived.

Conor O'Brien - Villagers

Forgive

Completely

November 1

Resentments

As smoking is to the lungs, so is resentment to the soul; even one puff is bad for you.

Elizabeth Gilbert

Resentments consume us, gnawing away at us, endlessly finding ways to make us feel awful. And the more we blame "them" for their actions, the stronger the poison becomes.

Oh, and who are we hurting? The person who has performed that vile deed? Or ourselves?

Do they even know what they are supposed to have done? More often than not, they have no idea that they've offended us.

So surely we want to discard our resentments so that we can get on with enjoying our lives?

Unfortunately, the idea of letting go of our resentment is something we refuse to consider until "they" have paid for their wickedness in full.

This attitude is madness. But if you're addicted to your pain, keep going with it.

If we want to move on and live comfortably, we want to forgive them completely and wholeheartedly.

So forgive. If you want to tell them you've forgiven them, beware, lest they do not feel they have done anything that needs forgiveness.

Forgiving is like taking a shower in a beautiful healing light and feeling all the angst drain from our body. Forgiveness is love and gentle joy.

Anger begets more anger, and forgiveness and love lead to more forgiveness and love.

Mahavira

Pleasing

I gotta stop treating people like I owe them something.

Tupac

If you try to please all, you please none.

Aesop

Are you trying to please everyone?

It is not possible. It only leads to inner and outer failure.

If we try to please everyone, we bounce from one thing to another, in constant turmoil.

When we start looking after ourselves and being honest about what we will or will not do, we probably ruffle other people's feathers.

Suddenly, we are no longer doing what they want anymore. They don't like it. So we will have a period of adjustment while they and you learn who the new you is.

But persevere. Become the person you are meant to be, who lives by the rules that come from your core. Be assertive. Be real.

Your relationships with everyone will be much better in the long run.

So much healthier.

Care about what other people think, and you will always be their prisoner.

Lao Tzu

Self-belief

Stop thinking you're doing it all wrong. Your path doesn't look like anybody else's because it can't, it shouldn't, and it won't.

Eleanor Brown

Whenever we feel like giving ourselves a hard time, all we have to do is to compare ourselves to others.

It is easy to spot those who have more, are better, smarter, wittier, and more attractive than us.

So easy to notice our faults and failings.

Comparing our inside to their outside. Seeing all the tokens of success that they flaunt, not considering for a moment that they are struggling too.

So much of their outward appearance is there to bolster their self-image and hide their inner demons.

If we step out of this inner turmoil and accept others as human beings with the same inner difficulties we do, we can spend our time in comfort with ourselves.

A flower does not think of competing with the flower next to it. It just blooms.

Zen Shin

November 4

Love

Do not feel lonely, the entire universe is inside you.

Rumi

Have you learnt to love yourself and to love others?
Think about it.
Really search for the answers.
And what are you going to do next?
Gentle inner peace.
A cloud of light that surrounds you, embraces you, makes everything alright. Clear and beautiful.
Gentle inner peace is such a magical hug.
Enjoy, no love, one's own company.
Delighting in the little things. Noticing the sunlight and the breeze on the petals and the water.
Stopping and taking time to be...
Loving.
Truly loving yourself.

Only if we understand will we care. Only if we care, will we help. Only if we help shall all be saved.

Jane Goodall

November 5

Seeing

We mostly see what we have learned to expect to see.

Betty Edwards

If you change your point of view, you see the world in a different way.

Lee Bacon

In the book "A Course in Miracles" it is suggested that we ask God (you can say universe), "Help me to see things differently."

More often than not, our state is one where we look at what happens to us as attacks. We expect people to take advantage of us, to do us down in one way or another.

We go into the world with our defence barriers up, expecting to have to attack or hide as each situation develops.

"Seeing things differently" changes all that. We go out viewing everyone as a friend, expecting good things to happen.

And when bad things do happen, we imagine they will lead to good things.

Now, I approach the world with joy and trust, which is what I get.

Above all, I wish to see.

Donna Goddard

The optimist sees the doughnut, the pessimist sees the hole.

Oscar Wilde

November 6

Respect

The great thing in the world is not so much to seek happiness as to earn peace and self-respect.

Thomas Huxley

Respect yourself. In all areas, in every way, respect yourself.

On a scale of 1-10, how are you doing with that at the moment?

If you were God, would you treat yourself differently?

How much time do you spend pointing out your failures and shortcomings to yourself? Saying to yourself, you should not have done or said that!

How much care do you take with what you eat, how much you exercise, and what you read or watch? Is there any honest self-respect there?

How do you treat the people you love? Or, for that matter, how do you treat others?

For we are all one. What we do or say to each other is what we do and say to ourselves.

Perhaps the surest test of an individual's integrity is his refusal to do or say anything that would damage his self-respect.

Thomas S Monson

I got my own back.

Maya Angelou

Dependency

Change begins when you realise that there are no hidden or buried treasures. No Santa Claus nor Genie. Just you and your determination to succeed.

Michael Bassey Johnson

We take so much for granted in our lives without giving it a thought.

Friends, love, comfort, belonging, acceptance, safety, security, availability of services for all our needs. Our health, our mental capacity, our doctors and hospitals.

Electricity, running water, heating, TV, internet, comfort! All there at our beck and call. Everything is catered for.

When something happens, and we lose anything in our lives, we feel so inadequate.

I discovered a leak in my utility room yesterday. Water splashing underfoot. (Worried emoji face) I had to turn my water off at the mains. (Thank God I found the stop cock)

I've arranged for a plumber to come today. But as I go to my bathroom basin, shower, and the kitchen sink, there is no water. Not even a gurgle!

And I realise how dependent I am on things that I do not have any control over.

And I wonder how many other areas in my life I am just mindlessly accepting without really being involved?

Are there relationships or friendships that I am not taking enough care of? Beware, and be on the lookout. Take action before you are forced to.

It can't be done for you; it must be done by you.

Frank Sonnenberg

November 8

Nothing

Enjoy the little things in life, for one day, you may look back and realise they were the big things.

Robert Breault

When I think back over the adventures and the loves in my life, it is the little things I remember.

I sailed a thirty-foot yacht from England to the Canary Islands, and my memory of it is the spray hitting my face as I squashed into a corner and steered through a storm.

Or the pink clouds roaring away over the horizon while the sun set. Or the feeling of warmth, love and connectedness as I sat in the cockpit with one of my companions. Simply being.

When I think of the loves in my life, it is a particular flower, song, or evening walk that resonates. My dog pushing at my arm when she wants my attention.

To try to recall more is too much.

So now I constantly notice the flower, the scent, or the breeze on the water to lock more moments into my existence.

A feeling of joy, if not shared or tasted, is a waste of a chance to be embraced.

Ana Claudia Antunes

Behaviour

The best way to capture moments is to pay attention. This is how we cultivate mindfulness.

Jon Kabat-Zinn

Pay attention!!!
What an outrageous suggestion!
Me?
Me! I do that, yes, YES, I do! I do!
Okay, well, occasionally, I allow my mind to wander.
Yes, I have looked at messages on my phone when in conversation with other people.
But doesn't everyone do that?
Or do they?
And even if they do, is that a justifiable excuse?
I don't know. You decide.
Well, actually, yes I do know for myself, but you will want to decide for yourself.
Do unto others...
Enjoy.

What you do with your attention is, in the end, what you do with your life.

John Green

Change

Change your thoughts, and you change your world.

Norman Vincent Peale

So easy to do if one does it.

However, we are set in our ways. Our way of life is easy. Even if it is hard or unpleasant, it requires no effort from us. It seems we just trudge on endlessly.

Whereas change! Well, change is going to be an effort! Surely it is... Even the very idea of doing something different is exhausting.

However, what if we started our change by just relaxing? Relaxing sounds fun and easy even. "Yes, I could relax" Then what?

So relax and allow the mind to empty itself, like water draining through a sieve. Then, perhaps, moving forward might seem easier to you.

Gently imagine something in your life being easier and more rewarding.

Choose that. Allow that into your life. Later, next time, or even before that, welcome some other easy way of being into your life.

Continue. Practice makes things possible.

What lies behind you and what lies in front of you, pales in comparison with what lies inside you.

Ralph Waldo Emerson

November 11

Thinking

Oh, how I've envied the lives of those who could spend life sitting down. A place to sit, a place to sit! I'd lament, circling my empty chair.

Wolfgang Hilbig

Thought after thought, fighting uselessly within us, like the tracks made in the thick, muddy water as we drive our boat onward toward an invisible, unknown destination.

We have so many useless thoughts that we can almost touch them. And their mass prevents us from seeing any answers.

It is not hard to stop, breathe, meditate, or allow some emptiness to wash the mud away.

Surely we can remember that.

Remembering that is not beyond our capabilities.

I think (too much), therefore I am (not there to live my life).

Thich Nhat Hanh

November 12

Realisation

*The internal war you wage with yourself may not be seen
by others but is always felt by you.*

Lorraine Nilon

An old Cherokee was teaching his grandson about life.

"Inside me, there is a terrible battle between two wolves. One is evil. He is anger, self-pity, guilt, resentment, false pride and ego.

The other is joy, peace, love, compassion, generosity, hope and kindness.

The same fight is going on inside you and everyone else!"

"Which one wins?" Asked his grandson.

The old man replied, "The one you feed."

"Rabbit's clever," said Pooh thoughtfully.
"Yes," said Piglet, "Rabbit's clever."
"And he has a brain."
"Yes," said Piglet, "Rabbit has a brain."
There was a long silence.
*"I suppose," said Pooh, "that that's why he never
understands anything."*

A A Milne

November 13

Sobriety

*Look, that's why there's rules, understand? So that you
think before you break 'em.*

Terry Pratchett

I am in AA. I haven't had a drink for quite a number of
years. Sometimes, friends talk about wanting to have a drink.
Or they go and have a drink without talking about it to
anyone. Many of those who pick up never manage to get
sober again.

I was thinking about this, about wanting to have a drink.
What does that mean? I believe it means they want to
change how they feel. They are not hoping for the wonders
that come with the "High" of being drunk. They know that
the high is a lie. It may come, but so fleetingly as to be
useless.

No, what they want is a change in their life. A change in
their behaviours. To check out and escape from the rules that
they and their immediate family bind them with. They can
no longer bear being strangled by themselves or others.

So it occurred to me that, rather than picking up a drink,
the road to freedom and happiness is to stop obeying the
rules. Refuse to be bound by them.

Decide who and what we want to be, announce it to the
world, and do it. Or instead, probably don't do it.

What is the worst that can happen? Whatever the worst
is, it is not as bad as the results of taking that drink. Picking
up that drink leads to insanity and death.

*Rules are for children. This is war, and in war, the only
crime is to lose.*

Joe Abercrombie

November 14

Loneliness

The time you feel lonely is the time you most need to be by yourself. Life's cruellest irony

Douglas Coupland

I think the loneliest, most damaging times in life are when we are with others but do not feel connected to them.

Times when we are being taken for granted. Which is, I think, a form of abuse. With no space for peace.

Like everything in life, there are degrees of this. Sometimes, our loneliness may only manifest as a tiny twang of discontent. But it is still there, gnawing away at our soul.

The steps to a solution are to recognise it before it worsens and then talk about it with an ally. All troubles grow and fester in secrecy.

I don't see how you can respect yourself if you must look in the hearts and minds of others for your happiness.

Hunter S Thompson

November 15

Learning

Nothing haunts us like the things we don't say.

Mitch Albon

Sometimes, the words make their way out of our mouths, and our chin slams shut before they can escape. We look at the words we hid and sometimes we even have a second go, but no.

And then we watch them go and make the mistakes we knew they would. The question we want to ask ourselves is, do they need to make the mistakes? Is that what was necessary for their growth? And more often than not, we find that is the case. We learn by living, not by avoiding.

We want to have the courage to "do" and let others "do" to discover what we need to learn.

Forgive yourself for not knowing what you didn't know before you learned it.

Maya Angelou

November 16

Uniqueness

What sets you apart can sometimes feel like a burden and it's not. And a lot of the time, it's what makes you great.

Emma Stone

We are all unique. One of our challenges or difficulties is wanting to be like others. We copy them when, in fact, copying doesn't work.

The push and pull we receive from social media and the feeling that we will never match up.

It is okay to be you!

Relax and enjoy being who you are. Feel proud of your differences. Embrace them fully.

We do not want to be like everybody else, or for that matter, like anybody else.

Enjoy being you!

Who you are authentically is alright.

Laverne Cox

November 17

Peace

*Wear the world like a loose garment, which touches us in a
few places and there lightly.*

St Francis of Assisi

It is too easy to be bogged down by our involvement in
the world and our endless doing, doing, doing.

It is so much better to let the world get on with the world.

Just elegantly gliding through our day, doing the little bit
assigned to us and letting the others fight over the rest of it.

Much better to leave it alone and allow it to run its course
while we find a way to have quiet peace.

Such a generous gift to give the world. Peace.

*Don't search for anything except peace. Try to calm the
mind. Everything else will come on its own.*

Baba Hari Das

Freedom

Lighthouses don't go running all over an island looking for boats to save; they just stand there shining.

Anne Lamott

Allow yourself the freedom to just be you.

You do not have to save the world.

You do not have to answer every call you get or go out looking for people to help.

Allow yourself to get on with your life in whatever way is more comfortable for you.

Do not be a slave or director. Do not do everything for them. Do not waste your time and energy trying to get them to do what you want them to do.

Learn to be. Learn to relax. Learn how to say "no." Learn how to say, "Do it however you want".

Learn that you are not responsible.

Have some peace and freedom. You deserve it.

It's not a matter of letting go – you would if you could. Instead of "Let it go," we should probably say, "Let it be."

Jon Kabat-Zinn

November 19

Being

Just be. Let your true nature emerge. Don't disturb your mind with seeking

Sri Nisargadatta Maharaj

And don't disturb your mind by thinking. Just sit for a moment and switch all your thoughts off. Be aware of your breathing.

Go into your heart with love.

And when you return, choose just one thing to focus on, to do, to accomplish.

Be calm

Have peace.

Enjoy

Life is not as serious as the mind makes it out to be.

Eckhart Tolle

The destination of life is this eternal moment.

Alan Watts

November 20

Gratitude

For him who has, more will be given, and he will have abundance; but for him who has not, even what he has will be taken away.

Matthew 13:12

I remember hearing that and thinking, "That's not fair" and then ignoring it.

Much later, I heard someone say that the quote was about gratitude. And that changed everything.

Now, I start my day with immense feelings of gratitude. I think of things and feel the gratitude for them in my body. I really experience it.

And my life has changed.

So much.

We get even more if we focus on the good in our lives and fill ourselves with gratitude for them. We get what we focus on.

If we constantly complain about our lives and focus on the lack, we continue to create and increase lack and negative things.

What we think, we create.

Acknowledging the good that you already have in your life is the foundation for all abundance.

Elkhart Tolle

The more you practice the art of thankfulness, the more you have to be thankful for.

Norman Vincent Peale

November 21

Self-belief

Sometimes the people around you won't understand your journey. They don't need to, it's not for them.

Joubert Botha

Sometimes, we want approval. We want encouragement and praise. We want people to notice us and what we do.

And when they don't understand or care what we are doing, we feel lonely. We question ourselves and our choices. We withdraw and may even think that we should do things differently and that we are in some way to blame.

But as the quote says, it's not their journey.

And most successful people have been misunderstood and questioned at some stage in their lives. But they kept going. They achieved what they set out to do, regardless of public opinion.

So hang in there! Keep going. Love yourself. Believe in yourself. Most importantly, enjoy what you are doing.

Do not let other people steal your dreams.

Make the most of yourself... for that is all there is of you.

Ralph Waldo Emerson

Relaxing

To have faith is to trust yourself to the water. When you swim, you don't grab hold of the water because if you do, you will sink and drown. Instead, relax and float.

Alan Watts

I have a friend who so desperately wants everything to be okay. So she constantly grabs everything, manipulating all her situations in the mistaken belief that she'll have control if she succeeds. And that if she had control, everything would be okay.

Her divorce gets worse and worse the more she tries to get what she wants out of it. And her oblivious husband goes on doing what he has always done. He doesn't care about anything. Doesn't listen to her. He agrees to things and then does what he planned to do anyway.

The more she struggles and fuels her hatred and anger, the worse she gets.

Incidentally, I know a man who is doing the same with his divorce, so this insanity is available to anyone.

She wants to learn to let go. To let her lawyers do their job and get on with living and relax with her life. What will happen will happen. Why persecute yourself before the event...

Like water that can clearly mirror the sky and the trees only so long as its surface is undisturbed, the mind can only reflect the true image of Self when it is tranquil and wholly relaxed.

Indra Devi

November 23

Fear

Your mind is biased.
And your brain is blind.
There's still a store of strength,
Left in you to find.

Charly Cox

Thank God we cannot properly remember the difficult, black times in our lives.

Yes, we may recall them, but not with the all-consuming power they had at the time.

The struggles. The no solution. The impossible. The unlovable. The hatred. The rage. The isolation. The doom. The fear.

They are all, of course, fear – all-consuming fear, wearing different clothes.

And when entirely in its grasp, it feels as though it is impossible that it can end.

And yet, both you and I know that it will. It can end sooner if we are prepared to go inside and access our peace within.

It is not always easy to do, but it is not impossible. We always have love inside. It may only be a pin-prick of light, but it is always there.

It is always there, and so I know – I will survive.

Oh no, not I, I will survive.
Oh, and as long as I know how to love, I know I'll stay alive.
I've got all my life to live.
And I've got all my love to give and I'll survive.
I will survive.
I will survive.

Dino Fekaris, Frederick J Perren

November 24

Expectations

We are where we are because we are what we are, and we are what we are because of our habitual thinking.

Catherine Ponder

Why settle for so little in life when you can have so much just by daring to be different in your thinking.

Catherine Ponder

What do you say about yourself? What are your expectations?

Are you trapped in the rut of "That's the way it's always been, and it always will be!"

Does your background, family, and upbringing chain you to a life and a world of lack and failure?

Stop for a moment and think about successful people. Are they only successful because their families are successful? Yes, some of them are, but the vast majority do not have overly successful backgrounds.

And there is a clue there.

What we focus on is what we bring into our lives.

It is our choice.

It is your choice.

What you praise, you increase.

Catherine Ponder

There is power in words. What you say is what you get.

Zig Ziglar

November 25

Judgement

When you judge another, you do not define them, you define yourself.

Wayne Dyer

There are two ways to go through life, either observing or judging.

When we observe, we experience what is going on. "This happened." "You did this." "I made this." We accept that as our experience, we get on with our lives without becoming emotionally involved.

But when we judge, we add our feelings and beliefs to what happened, "This happened, and it made me feel angry..." "She managed to train for a marathon while working full-time, and with three kids under five..." "OMG, what does she look like in those jeans? I hope I don't look like that."

As soon as we add judgement to our observations, we create a roadblock in our lives. We start to run scared, harbour anger or seek revenge and creep away and hide.

It is so good to stop judging. The moment we step away from it and get on with our lives, we can feel good about ourselves.

Refuse to live under a pall of negative emotion.

Be curious, not judgemental.

Walt Whitman

November 26

Peace

You may say I'm a dreamer,
But I'm not the only one.
I hope someday you'll join us,
And the world will live as one.

John Lennon

I didn't know how to get the information from my heart, my inner being, or, as some say, my higher self. I lived in a state of emotional turmoil, at battle with myself and the world, dominated by my ego.

I tried to go inside and contact my heart, but the struggle to do that often made it impossible.

Then someone or something whispered to me that the only thing God wanted for me, for all of us, was peace.

Peace. Now, I had something to focus on. Something to choose. Something to embrace. Whatever happened in my life, I could learn to switch it off and choose peace. Feel the peace that is always within me flooding through me.

Search for ways to bring peace into your life.

Peace.

How simple.

How obtainable.

How liberating.

How incredibly wonderful.

Nothing can bring you peace but yourself.

Ralph Waldo Emerson

November 27

Worry

*If the problem can be solved, why worry? If the problem
cannot be solved, worrying will do you no good.*

Shantideva

Ah, the joys of worry. Inflicting pain upon ourselves before it happens!

Worry is fear.

Worry has never prevented anything from going wrong. It has only robbed us of peace of mind and joy.

Our ego may trick us into thinking that worrying will protect us from disaster, but it won't.

Just consider your past worries for a moment. How many of them went badly, or as badly as you invented them going?

So, experiment with this. Think of what you are worrying about, and say, "I trust that this will go okay."

You don't need to imagine the details. You trust that everything will work out alright.

Go forward in your mind to a time after the event and imagine it having gone well.

Then relax.

And enjoy.

Trust yourself. You know more than you think you do.

Benjamin Spock

November 28

Never

It is never too late to be what you might have been.

George Eliot

Don't say "Never" or "Never again."

Don't block possibilities from your life. Be open to experiences.

"Never" limits your thinking, is judgemental, and belittles you.

Yes, there are experiences we have that we may not want to repeat. But never is slamming doors on opportunities.

We want to go through our lives with an open attitude and a gentle sense of adventure.

Explore.

Take risks.

Live.

Enjoy.

If you do what you love, you'll never work a day in your life.

Marc Anthony

November 29

Adventure

Believe in yourself and all that you are. Know that there is something inside you that is greater than any obstacle.

Christian D Larson

Life is a mystery. Sometimes, it seems to run smoothly along, with no upsets, but we know, if we think back, that the unexpected is not far away.

Sometimes, our boring and repetitive life seems to drag on for so long that we find ourselves wishing for a bit more mystery in our lives.

Then, there are times when one mystery or unexpected event after another keeps appearing, overwhelming us.

No sooner have we recovered from a puncture, when the road closes. Someone bumps into us, and cows are wandering around on the road. Too much, too much!

Rather than collapsing in despair, embrace them all with excitement. Open your arms in anticipation of the next adventure. Live life to the full.

It's better than dying slowly in front of your television, not missed by anyone.

The world is a book, and those who do not travel read only one page.

Saint Augustine

November 30

Difference

*Everyone can do simple things to make a difference, and
every little bit really does count.*

Stella McCartney

Making a difference. Taking those extra few seconds to consider what we say. Deciding to hold out our hand and to be there. Choosing to do the slightly harder thing, because we know it is the right thing. Genuinely listening and then thoughtfully replying.

All of them and pages more of ways to make a difference.

Although the real beneficiary of it all is ourselves, when we do whatever is necessary to make a difference, however vast or minor, we are the ones who benefit so much. We can walk, talk, and smile with ourselves, being encompassed in the glow that goes with it.

How wonderful. Surely, no sane person would ever refuse an opportunity to make a difference?

*We can change the world and make it a better place. It is in
your hands to make a difference.*

Nelson Mandela

Be

Open

December 1

Experience

*A man who carries a cat by the tail learns something he can
learn in no other way.*

Mark Twain

We choose what kind of day we have and what we will
experience.

That statement may seem extraordinary and even
nonsensical. We look at what life throws at us and throw up
our hands.

How can I choose what kind of day I'll have when "all"
this is happening to me? I'm sinking, and swimming is not
an option. In fact, drowning seems like quite a pleasant
alternative to this. At least I would have peace!

But we do have a choice. We always do, though we may
not realise it or claim our choice.

In my inner being, there is always peace. A gentle pool of
love and calm waiting for us to bathe in it.

When we let our ego, shouting insanities, lead us into any
event, even nice ones, it can find ways to destroy us.

If we approach any situation, however awful it may
appear, and allow our inner voice to guide us, it becomes
okay.

So I choose peace. Not always; I am human. Sometimes I
allow the shit to overwhelm me, but never for long, for when
the pain rings its bell, I kick my ego out and choose peace.

Nothing ever becomes real until it is experienced.

John Keats

December 2

Doubt

The moment you doubt whether you can fly, you cease forever to be able to do it.

J M Barrie – Peter Pan

It is essential to guard oneself against doubts and discard them wherever they poke their head above the sand.

We want to continue believing in ourselves, no matter the challenges.

If we can do something once, we can do it again. And we can do it better each time and enjoy it.

Our ego wants us to doubt, and it wants us to fail. The more miserable we are, the more control it has over us.

By doing things, challenging ourselves, and feeding our self-belief whenever we can, we are growing and becoming more able – more in control of ourselves and our future.

We have not failed if we do not achieve what we set out to do. We have gathered feedback.

Go out, do, live, enjoy!

If you have built castles in the air, your work need not be lost; that is where they should be. Now, put the foundations under them.

Henry David Thoreau

December 3

Reality

*When wealth is lost, nothing is lost; when health is lost,
something is lost; when character is lost, all is lost.*

Billy Graham

Your mind is a magnet. Constantly pulling everything and anything into itself and then creating that as your reality.

Also, beware of where you take it. Take care about what you let it near. Consider the things you watch and read. Is it what you want in your life?

If you are addicted to soap operas, your mind will do its best to recreate the awfulness in your life.

If you engage endlessly with the news, the attacks, the rapes, the unspeakable things that are happening out there, your mind is trying to find ways to make you suffer too.

Watch the parts of the news you need for your work, perhaps once a day and switch off what you do not need to hear.

Enjoy living a life that expects peace, love, and calm as the norm.

Have peace. Enjoy

*You should feel beautiful, and you should feel safe. What
you surround yourself with should bring you peace of mind
and peace of spirit.*

Stacy London

Stopping

Life is not as serious as the mind makes it out to be.

Eckhart Tolle

Don't take life too seriously. We are only here once, so we want to do the best we can to make our experiences and the experiences of our fellow travellers as good as possible.

So many people spend their lives struggling. Struggling to do their best and make everything right, and struggling to take responsibility for everything.

STOP.

YES STOP!

Take a breath and take it easy. Look for ways to make your life easier, better, simpler, and more relaxed. Stop trying to get everyone else to do the "right" things.

Let go.

Take it easy.

STOP.

You don't have to be perfect. Nor do they. And your attempts to make them perfect are doomed before you even start. That is just a lie that you are perpetuating.

STOP.

Enjoy

We will be more successful in all our endeavours if we can let go of the habit of running all the time, and take little pauses to relax and re-centre ourselves. And we'll also have a lot more joy in living.

Thich Nhat Hanh

December 5

Impatience

Hostile to the past, impatient of the present, and cheated of the future, we were much like those whom men's justice, or hatred, forces to live behind prison bars.

Albert Camus

People are so impatient. We are all so impatient. We want perfection now from everyone and ourselves.

And, of course, "they" all want perfection too. The trouble is that their perfection is not ours, so we clash. We feel agitated and hard done by, but then so do they.

The truth is that we cannot control other people, and when we try to, it causes everyone pain, except, of course, our ego, which relishes in the turmoil it can create.

Our inner voice, our inner spirit will happily guide us to achieving peace. However, it cannot guarantee that things will be the way we would like.

But when offered the choice of being right and having peace, the sane choice is always to have and create peace.

Don't search for anything except peace. Try to calm the mind. Everything else will come on its own.

Baba Hari Das

December 6

Perception

We cannot solve our problems with the same thinking we used when we created them.

Albert Einstein

Would our lives be flat and boring if we had no problems? No, surely not. The idea of having peace of mind seems an impossibility for so many. Their problems zing off each other like crazy balls in a pinball machine when you shoot in several balls at once.

No sooner has one problem or challenge kicked us in the face when another smashes into us, followed by yet another.

Surely, to allow this is madness. "But I can't help it! I don't want to feel like this! All my problems are real!"

"Help" is a useless word because they are incapable of listening anymore. They are so bound to their troubles.

If we can help them to focus on just one of them, we can guide them towards peace and sanity. None of the worries, however awful, are as bad as they could be. Peel away the layers of that one problem. Yes, just that one.

Then, when you have some solution, the next one will be easier to undress.

If you believe it'll work out, you will see opportunities. If you believe it won't work out, you'll see obstacles.

Wayne Dyer

December 7

Stillness

*Learning how to be still, to really be still and let life happen
– that stillness becomes a radiance.*

Morgan Freeman

Stillness is an entirely foreign idea to so many people. They dash, they indulge, they talk. They have no idea how to exist without noise.

Intoxicated by the rubbish that pours into them, whether through their phone, games console, or TV.

Most public spaces play us music. Presumably, they are worried about how we would cope if we encountered silence.

How often do you go and sit in nature? Just you and nature alone. Communing with the stillness, emptying our souls and honestly nourishing ourselves.

Do you want to make a date now?

Be still. Stillness reveals the secrets of eternity.

Lao Tzu

December 8

Judgement

My judgements prevent me from seeing the good that lies behind appearances.

Wayne Dyer

Acceptance or judgement,
Which is the norm that you travel through life with.
As you walk down the street, do you see ugly, fat, shabby, self-absorbed, proud, superior, snob, rude, sloppy, lazy, given up, etc., people walking down the road towards you? Please feel free to add your list of adjectives.

Or do you walk down the road filled with love? Smiling at everyone. Giving them loving thoughts, wishing them well, and happiness. Do you engage and say "lovely day" to them? Do you spread love and kindness wherever you go?

Before passing judgment on somebody, just give it a thought about what he or she went through.

Grenville Kleiser

December 9

Being

I am the one I was looking for in everyone else. I have been led back home to my heart and higher power.

Angela Hughes

Coming home to oneself. And so many of us have no idea that is possible. That we might find the love and peace we yearn for within ourselves.

We have spent so long searching for something that was not there. Doing, buying, ingesting, arguing, critiquing, blaming in our attempt to fill the hole, the void we feel within ourselves.

We grab one form of pain after another, in the grip of our ego, unable to stop and allow peace to embrace us.

There is peace in our heart. But when we tell others this, they slam their minds shut. They say things to themselves like, "It's okay for you. You haven't got shit like mine. You're special. And actually, I suspect you're lying."

All that without a conscious effort.

But we are all one. If I can have peace. If I can think with my heart. If I can allow the disasters to float past me without being sucked into their insanity. If I can, then you can too. It's just a choice.

Peace comes from within. Do not seek it without.

Buddha

December 10

Peace

My shadow said to me, "What if I told you that I am your soul?"

Michael Bassey Johnson

It's all in the mind.

George Harrison

How wonderful peace and calm are. So all-encompassing. So freeing.

And yet, so many of us cannot remember the last time we had any prolonged experience of peace.

Something is always in the way, bubbling its fumes and preventing us from enjoying it.

The culprits? Anger and control. They flare up and fill us with their bile before we have even had a moment to think about it.

Yet, there is always a moment. If we say or ask, "Help me to see things differently".

Then, pause and allow the peaceful way to flow gently into us.

Then there is peace.

Look at everything as though you are seeing it for the first or the last time, then your time on earth will be filled with glory.

Betty Smith

December 11

Control

Two things define you: your patience when you have nothing and your attitude when you have everything.

George Bernard Shaw

I think that our patience and our attitude define us wherever we are. If we do not have patience, everything very quickly gets out of control.

And our attitude and ability to face any situation in a balanced way is vital. When we are suffering from any form of discomfort, it is because we are indulging in expectations that do not benefit us. We are trying to control the world, other people and ourselves. We arc failing, and we suffer.

We are not meant to control any of them. We are like Sisyphus, endlessly rolling a boulder up a steep hill, and watching it roll back down every night.

Let go.

Recognising that you are not where you want to be is a starting point to begin changing your life.

Deborah Day

December 12

Freedom

*You have a treasure within you that is infinitely greater
than anything the world can offer.*

Eckhart Tolle

Christmas approaches and people have put out their lights and decorations. One of my neighbours has an inflatable Father Christmas that has a leak. Sometimes, he stands, proud and full. At other times, he subsides into a red and white sadness.

It occurred to me, after watching his comings and goings, that is how many of us are.

We inflate and deflate. When deflated, we more easily become prey to our insane ego.

(In case you think your ego is not insane, I would like to suggest that all egos are insane, with a desire to make us struggle.)

The simple way to help us stay inflated is to meditate. It does not have to take up a lot of time. But it is an essential guard against deflation and the negative thoughts and behaviour that assail us when we do not meditate.

*The secret to happiness is freedom... and the secret to
freedom is courage.*

Thucydides

December 13

Rising

For the human soul is virtually indestructible, and its ability to rise from the ashes remains as long as the body draws breath.

Alice Miller

As a phoenix dies, it bursts into flames, and from the ashes, a new bird, a new phoenix, rises in full glory.

And so it is with us if we can but realise it. From our disasters, from our unbearable trials, we rise. Maybe not immediately, but in due course, we rise again.

Richer, wiser, and stronger because of what we have been through. It is our trial that gives us our strengths and qualities.

Do not despair as you struggle through your difficulties. Harness some of your future strengths to carry you through.

Life tried to crush her, but only succeeded in creating a diamond.

John Mark Green

December 14

Forgiveness

It's toughest to forgive ourselves. So it's probably best to start with other people. It's almost like peeling an onion. Layer by layer, forgiving others, you really do get to the point where you can forgive yourself.

Patty Duke

It was a long, slow journey. So much time was spent clinging to the things that seemed "impossible" to forgive.

And then, when one of them was genuinely forgiven and moved on from. I arrived in a world and a state of mind where that truly did not matter anymore, forgiven. Peace is left, genuine peace and comfort, a feeling of "how can I get more of this?"

So then, I hunted out the next stupid revenge thought. Finding and caringly forgiving.

What a magical joy.

Unbelievable.

We may not know how to forgive, and we may not want to forgive, but the very fact we are willing to forgive begins the healing practice.

Louise Hay

December 15

Fear

Feel the fear and do it anyway.

Susan Jeffers

Let's talk about fear for a moment. It grips us. It surrounds us. It drags us into an inescapable place. It can even immobilise us. Presenting itself as unending.

But it cannot prevent us from thinking.

It may tell us that it can, but it cannot. We can still think. We can still choose what we think.

We can breathe. Fear has never stopped you breathing. If it had, you wouldn't be reading this.

So breathe. Concentrate on your breathing. Nothing else.

Fear tells you there is an impenetrable wall in front of you. This is not true. It is just fear trying to control you.

So remember to breathe. Concentrate on your breathing. Think slowly and calmly about what it is that you feel fear about. Nearly all, if not all, of the fear is a lie. Thinking calmly now, you can understand that it is a lie.

Decide to think about things without fear. If the fear reappears, repeat the process.

Fear is a lie.

Fears are nothing more than a state of mind.

Napoleon Hill

Struggles

I've got a hard road to travel
And a rough rough way to go
Said it's a hard road to travel
And a rough rough way to go.

Jimmy Cliff

Our roads always seems to be "our" road. As we struggle on, it is difficult to imagine that others have ever travelled it before. It feels that nobody could ever have had our experiences.

Our ego clutches the pain so tightly, blinding us from help. "There cannot be help!" it screams. "I am alone."

When we meet people who say they went through something like this and survived, we don't believe them.

"Let the pain bury me completely."

When we think about our past, remembering struggles we have managed to find a way through, we greet them with a "Yah, but this time's different. This is worse. Shut up while I revel in my pain!"

But if you decide to be honest with yourself, you know, without a shadow of a doubt, that "This Too Shall Pass." This will end.

You will survive. And you do not need to choose to drown in pain as it is happening. You can choose to relax and know that we need all our experiences to become the person we are destined to be.

I dream of a home far beyond the sea,
Where there is love and peace and joy for me.
Oh, in my eyes, I see troubles and dangers for me.
But destiny where it leads me, I must go, hey.

Jimmy Cliff

December 17

Rubbish

*We are not cisterns made for hoarding, we are channels
made for sharing.*

Billy Graham

What have you got stuffed into the back of cupboards,
waiting for your children to throw away or sell on eBay?

How much junk have you got that you don't need and is
dragging you down with its unspoken existence?

Do yourself a favour and start to get rid of it now.

*The garbage can is for things that have no importance. If it
did have some value, it no longer has any.*

J R Rim

December 18

Mistakes

It takes guts and humility to admit mistakes. Admitting we're wrong is courage, not weakness.

Roy T Bennet

Oh dear.
"Come on," I say to myself, "Be brave."
And so I fess up, and it feels much better.
My mother used to admire it in me, and it's still there, unlike my brother, who would never admit anything, even when his denial was so absolutely obviously a lie.
And so, as we go through life, we can choose the right thing to do.
Hurrah for that.

Be not ashamed of mistakes and thus make them crimes.

Confucius

Laughing at our mistakes can lengthen our own life. Laughing at someone else's can shorten it.

Cullen Hightower

December 19

Conversations

*A real conversation is an adventure into the unfamiliar
where two people present their authentic self, unguarded
and welcoming the uncertain.*

Mel Schwartz

Do you interrupt people when they talk to you, or do you wait for them to finish, wait in silence for a moment or two, before replying?

So many people cannot wait for the other person to stop before pushing their views out there.

So many people stop listening to the other person after the first few words.

So many people have no idea how to listen to anyone.

So many people are the most important person in the world.

Very few people honestly engage in conversation with concern and love.

Can you learn to be one of them?

*I haven't spoken to my wife in years. I didn't want to
interrupt her.*

Rodney Dangerfield.

December 20

Respect

I have no right, by anything I do or say, to demean a human being in his own eyes. What matters is not what I think of him; it is what he thinks of himself. To undermine a man's self-respect is a sin.

Antoine de Saint-Exupéry

People say "cringe" to others or themselves. Requesting that the recipient wallow in the shame, the acute embarrassment of their act or thought.

What an appalling thing to do. What a dreadful suggestion. What a poisonous slur.

Why would you choose to direct yourself or anyone else to embrace such a pitiful state?

Do not use it.

Cast cringe out of your vocabulary. Never use it again!

It is not a word that someone of your calibre should ever entertain. If you cannot say something uplifting, be silent. If someone says it to you, say no thank you…

Our self-respect does not have a price tag.

Nawaz Sharif

December 21

Caring

One of the deep secrets of life is that all that is really worth the doing is what we do for others.

Lewis Carrol

The things we do for ourselves, the stuff we buy, the distractions we use are just that. Temporary distractions. They do not make us feel fulfilled.

Of course, if we are only doing things for others grudgingly or because we "have" to, it does not give us the benefits we enjoy when we are totally selfless.

It is not a good thing to spoil our good deeds by wishing that we didn't have to do them.

Selfless gifts of our time and love make us feel quietly good without even thinking about it.

So give your time and love and reap your unexpected rewards.

Too often, we underestimate the power of a touch, a smile, a kind word, a listening ear, an honest compliment, or the smallest act of caring, all of which have the potential to turn a life around.

Leo Buscaglia

Living

*When I think of all the good times
that I've wasted having good times.
When I think of all the good times
That's been wasted having good times.*

The Animals

Just consider for a moment the amount of time you have frittered away doing mindless things.

Yes, you needed to waste time when you were young. You needed to experiment and make mistakes to discover who you were. That's how we grow up.

Most people die in their mid-twenties, and they spend the next forty years waiting for their bodies to catch up and die.

That is the greatest mistake we can make. We slam the door on adventure and embrace mindless routine. We enter the stage where we are wasting times (not good times) on having no times.

Forever.

Go out.

Take risks.

Live and laugh. And cry, too. Allow your emotions to flood through you.

Don't fear death, but rather the unlived life.

Natalie Babbitt

December 23

Trust

Being able to feel safe with other people is probably the single most important aspect of mental health: safe connections are fundamental to meaningful and satisfying lives.

Bessel Van der Kolk

It is so wonderful to be able to sit with someone we trust and talk honestly. Knowing that whatever is said goes no further.

We all want to find someone we can do that with. More importantly we all want to be that trustworthy person.

No gossip for us.

Gossip kills.

It may entertain briefly, but the damage it can cause is unspeakable.

Trust and be trustworthy.

Share and grow.

Being trustworthy requires: Doing the right thing and doing things right.

Don Peppers

December 24

Mind

*Your mind can be either your prison or your palace. What
you make it, is yours to decide.*

Bernard Kelvin Clive

Prison or Palace?
Not a difficult choice, one would think.
And yet, so many people choose prison. They allow their
ego to run riot through their lives. Constantly digging up
rancid, putrid pieces of their past to abuse and torment them
with. They find people from their past who can verify and
magnify their warped view of everything.
They condemn and blame themselves and all the other
parties involved to drown in their cancerous bitterness.
If they think of the future, they magnify every catastrophe
they can imagine.
All their conversations are embellished with bitterness
and hatred.
The concept of forgiveness to them is an impossibility.
And this is the world they are choosing to create.
What, I wonder, would happen if they moved from the
past and the future into the stillness of the present? Now.
The now can be as wonderful, peaceful, and joy-filled as
we choose to accept it. From their perspective, the only
shortcoming is that it contains no pain.

*The attitude of faith is to let go and become open to truth,
whatever it might turn out to be.*

Alan Watts

December 25th

Thoughts

But where do you go to, my lovely
When you're alone in your bed?
Tell me the thoughts that surround you
I want to look inside your head, yes, I do.

Peter Sarstedt

Regardless of my day, good or bad, there used to be a stampede of thoughts just waiting to fight for ownership of my brain the moment my head hit the pillow.

I say "there used to be" because they are no longer as bad as they were.

Stampede is a good word to describe what they do as they fight to the top, slashing through anything that gets in their way.

Some, a few, were genuine causes for worry and fear. Enough to freeze the strongest of us. But many are just mundane thoughts about sending an email. A merry-go-round of insanity determined to keep me awake. Determined.

I now switch on a meditation before I start to go to sleep, and if I can keep my mind focused on listening to it, my thoughts do not trouble me.

I also have a to-do list, and I say to myself, "I don't need to think about that now, it's on my list."

I spend my life, day, and waking hours focused, as far as possible, on positive things.

I avoid the negatives.

Ruthlessly.

Life's too short. Anything could happen, and it usually does, so there is no point sitting around thinking about the ifs, ands, and buts.

Amy Winehouse

Feelings

Is it really possible to tell someone else what one feels?

Leo Tolstoy

Feelings cannot kill you.

And often, we do not even know what the feeling we are having is.

Something happens in our body. A feeling. And we do not honestly know what it means. Is it sorrow, fear, envy, jealousy, inadequacy?

We grab a name and a label that seems to fit and say, "I feel lonely."

We think, "I don't like feeling like this. What can I do to change the way I feel?"

And often, our solution is to turn to the addiction we have chosen as the best sop to drown the feeling in.

We may ask ourselves what the cause of the feeling is, "He left me", or "She laughed at me", or "I'm ugly." Then, we do very little to address the cause, and we pull the feeling closer to us. Ensuring that it won't escape.

We can, however, change the feeling if we choose. Reject the first one that crept up on us and say, "I don't want to feel like this. I am not going to. I am going to choose to be okay. I will choose to feel positive about the world and my life."

Don't let negatives drown you. Choose to be in control of yourself and your life.

It's often just enough to be with someone. I don't need to touch them. Not even talk. A feeling passes between you both. You're not alone.

Marilyn Monroe

December 27

The Beast

The beast in me
Has had to learn to live with pain.

Johnny Cash

God help the beast in me.

Johnny Cash

Thank God, by and large, I have subdued the beast in me.

And if I have, then it must be possible, for I know I am not special and different.

For a long time, he ruled the majority of my life, totally uncontrollable.

I wreaked havoc wherever I went. I had a powerful beast.

Most people are not faced with such a monster, but they still have their beast, their inner demons, who easily cause damage to themselves and anyone they can attack.

The beast is ego-driven. Looking for any weakness it can exploit.

In our heart lies the angelic power and voice of peace, calm and love. Allowing our thoughts to drop down from our heads to our hearts changes them instantly.

You can do this now and discover that this is true. Everything in us changes.

And from there, we can walk freely. Suddenly, the stepping stones that cross the raging water appear, and we can walk easily and comfortably on.

Your inner peace is the greatest and most valuable treasure
that you can discover.

Akiroq Brost

December 28

Deception

Mundus vult decipi: The world wants to be deceived.

Walter Kaufman

Reality is too frightening to behold, so we accept and hide in the falsehoods we are fed.

Sops, pieces of bread in warm milk, to keep us quiet.

The "Authorities" looking after themselves, while the masses go mindlessly along with what they are offered.

Only by living within ourselves can we have freedom and peace of mind. Meditation and stillness are the keys to life.

Even though we are deceived, still believe. Though we are betrayed, still forgive. Love completely, even those who hate you.

Sun Myung Moon

We are never deceived; we deceive ourselves.

Johann Wolfgang von Goethe

December 29

Emotions

Well, we all need someone we can lean on.
And if you want it, you can lean on me.

Keith Richards/Mick Jagger

We all need someone we can lean on. All of us. I do, and you do. The difficulty, if you want to call it that, is finding the person we can lean on.

And then there is the problem, if you want to call it that, of when we lean too long, too hard, and take advantage.

If I am leaning on you, then I must allow you to lean on me, too.

The worst thing in life is when other person removes themselves, when they are no longer prepared to let us lean on them. They may still be here physically, but mentally and emotionally, they've gone.

When this happens, probably the best thing to do is to leave as well. Leave altogether. Otherwise, we end by giving ourselves away entirely until nothing is left. We are empty. We become a vacuum.

I am not so different in my history of abandonment from anyone else after all. We have all been split away from the earth, each other, ourselves.

Susan Griffin

December 30

Acceptance

When you think everything is someone else's fault, you will suffer a lot. When you realise that everything springs only from yourself, you will learn both peace and joy.

Dalai Lama

Even when we are not blaming others, our ego is probably searching for ways to convince us that it is "their fault".

If we can only realise that and decide to let go of our troubles, we can have peace and even joy.

Very few of our troubles are happening now. We are just keeping them alive with worry, resentment, hatred and fear. Surely, if we can realise and accept that, then letting go of them would be a sensible decision.

If we are suffering pain, it is because we are choosing to.

Don't let the behaviour of others destroy your inner peace.

Dalai Lama

December 31

Letting Go

It is by self-forgetting that one finds.
It is by forgiving that one is forgiven.
It is by dying that one awakens to eternal life.

St Francis of Assisi

We want to learn to let go. We want to learn to stop trying to run the world and ourselves. We want to accept life as it happens. We want to stop fighting and surrender.

Only when we let go and stop blindly searching will we find. And there will be peace, calm and serenity.

It is only by forgiving that we can achieve forgiveness. We can never have peace, calm, or serenity until we have finally succeeded in forgiving ourselves. Lack of self-forgiveness is a boulder attached to a hangman's noose, which we wear around our neck.

Letting go of life, dying, is no longer dying as we have thought of it. Dying is going home to the peace and calm and serenity which we return to being only a soul. We are no longer burdened by the restrictions of our human body.

If you have a sister and she dies, do you stop saying you have one? Or are you always a sister, even when the other half of the equation is gone?

Jodi Picoult

Made in the USA
Monee, IL
04 May 2026

49510322R00216

Made in the USA
Monee, IL
04 May 2026

49510322R00216